IT'S ALL RELATIVE

How To Create Your Own Personal

Family History Trivia Game

By Lynn Bonsey and Lorna Healey

Entertainment

AWARDS

Weddings

HOME SWEET HOME

SPORTS

dates

HOBBIES

WITHDRAWN STATISTICS

HERITAGE BOOKS, INC.

Copyright 1988 By
Lynn Bonsey and Lorna Healey

Text illustrations by Christine Amell Richards

Published 1988 By

HERITAGE BOOKS, INC.
1540E Pointer Ridge Place, Bowie, Maryland 20716
(301)-390-7709

ISBN 1-55613-148-8

QUESTION: Why is this book dedicated to our family?

ANSWER: Because they inspired us to create *IT'S ALL RELATIVE*, both as a legacy, and as a tribute to our family's special bond of love.

TABLE OF CONTENTS

List of Figures

CHAPTER 1

Introduction

If you want to create a priceless family keepsake, one which you and your family can share and enjoy now, and one which future generations will cherish, then *IT'S ALL RELA-TIVE* is for you.

As sisters, we developed this game for one reason: to create a unique gift for our parents. But in this process of sorting memorabilia, studying our family history, and sharing our memories, we realized we were doing much more than creating an unusual gift.

By researching, reminiscing, and writing about our family, we knew we'd learn more about our roots. However, we never expected to learn so much, not only about our family's history, but about ourselves, and our places in that history.

Sometimes we surprised each other when we discovered we didn't share the same recollection or perspective about an incident. Occasionally, we disagreed on an answer to a family trivia question. Frequently, our memories prompted lengthy, sentimental discussions of what used to be. But we always had lots of fun, and very little trouble, creating countless questions about the most important group of people in our lives - our family.

We've written this book so you, too, can discover that a family is much more than people of common ancestry - it's a unique group of people who share common experiences, lineage, laughter, and love.

CHAPTER 2

Getting Started

What is family trivia?

At first glance it may not make sense to pair "family", surely the most important group in the world, with "trivia", generally defined as unimportant matters.

But think about it. One person's idea of trivia may be a vital part of another person's life. For instance, you may not particularly care that the Smiths' cat was hit and killed by a car, but to the Smiths, this apparently trivial matter is a family tragedy.

Or it may not mean much to you that our father, Osmond Clark Bonsey, was named for his uncle, also Osmond Clark Bonsey, who died at the young age of 22 from tuberculosis, but to our father and us, this is relevant and intriguing.

On a lighter side, think about trivia as it relates to *you* on a daily basis. How long do you spend in the shower? What do you eat for breakfast? How far do you drive to work? Which co-worker do you dislike? What's the first thing you do upon arriving home from work?

And in a historical sense: When, where, and how did your parents meet? What was your paternal grandmother's maiden name? What state did your ancestors first settle? What ancestor served in the Civil War? How many nationalities do your ancestors represent?

The answers to all these questions are trivial details, but remember, details make up the larger story. And each family's details, those seemingly insignificant facts, tell a different story. As you research your roots, and then use this information to write your version of *IT'S ALL RELATIVE*, your family's story will come alive.

Do I need special qualifications to create *IT'S ALL RELATIVE*?

Creating *IT'S ALL RELATIVE* is easy. You don't need any special qualifications, skills, or talents. Anyone – grandparent, parent, young adult, or adolescent – can create this game for his or her family. And, although it's easier and more fun if two people initially research and write the game together as we did, writing it alone can also be a rewarding endeavor.

It's all a matter of deciding what will work best for you and your family. To that end, we hope this book's suggestions and guidelines will inspire you to create your own game.

Do I have to use each step in this book?

We've designed this book as a "guide" for you to pursue your personal family trivia and history. You do not have to use all of our suggested search and research techniques, nor do you have to complete them in any particular order. However, we urge you to read the entire book before beginning because it will give you an overview of the many choices you have as you research and write your game.

To help you plan and organize your game as efficiently and easily as possible, we've written this book just as we created our own game: step-by-step, gradually expanding our focus. Consequently, each chapter stands on its own, yet builds on the previous chapter. For instance, we started by "brainstorming" (CHAPTER 4) because our original intent was strictly to create an amusing Christmas present for our parents. Basically we wrote our questions and answers from our earliest recollections, moving chronologically through our lives.

But as we discussed several of these anecdotes and events, we concluded there were lots of unanswered questions which we couldn't answer without interviewing our relatives and doing further research into family records and memorabilia. We quickly realized that although using these research techniques meant much more work, our game and our knowledge of our family's history would be greatly enhanced by doing so.

Because we eventually incorporated a historical timeline (CHAPTER 5), searched our family archives and treasures (CHAPTER 8), researched primary and secondary public records (CHAPTER 7), and included part of our family tree

(CHAPTER 6), as well as brainstormed our memories, our family's game now focuses on both current and past history, and its tone varies from lighthearted to serious, with questions ranging from: When Lynn and Lorna were each nine months pregnant, what was their combined weight?, to: What caused Richard McGraw's death?

If you follow our suggested step-by-step procedures, your game will be comprehensive and detailed. Even if you choose to skip some steps, your game will still be a valuable addition to your family history.

What are my research options?

As the game's creator, you have several options. You may choose to focus on current family history; that is, to write questions revolving around your lifetime and your living relatives. And you may decide to do little formal research beyond brainstorming your memories.

Or you may choose to use some informal records and memorabilia from your family archives to include data that reaches back a couple of generations.

You may even opt to focus your game on your genealogical background researching primary sources and creating more of a formal, informational game.

You'll have to make each of these decisions based on your personal needs. Time is certainly a factor, as is the size and location of your family; and the amount and availability of materials. It's not necessary to determine the focus of your game before you begin your research - although your task may be easier, in terms of organization, if you do so.

Can I write the game alone?

You certainly can research and write your game by yourself. However, we encourage you to work with a family member if possible because your common family history will help you develop a more creative and comprehensive game than you could on your own. As sisters, writing both the game and this book enriched our already close relationship. It's an experience we wouldn't have missed.

Do I have to complete all the research before playing the game?

No. In a sense, your family history game will never be complete because you can continue to add questions to it as new events occur, and as you discover further information. (Players also have opportunities to add questions during the game as explained in CHAPTER 12.) However, you will want to have researched enough information, and written enough questions and answers to make *IT'S ALL RELATIVE* interesting the first time you and your family play.

What if I want the game to be a surprise gift?

You can work with one person, as we did, and still gather enough information for your game to be a surprise for others in your family. There's no harm in telling family members you're researching your roots and family trivia; in fact, many of them will be eager to help you. Then you can combine their information with yours and surprise them with the game.

How do I choose my game's categories?

CHAPTER 3: Selecting Categories, explains in detail your many options for category selection. In brief, you should choose at least four categories - for example Entertainment, Statistics, Sports, Miscellaneous - with the option to choose up to eight different categories for your game. It may be helpful for you to determine your categories before you start your research so you can key your research to them; but there are also advantages to gathering key information and classifying it into categories later. As Chapter 3 explains, it depends on your needs.

What materials do I need and how do I organize them?

Your key to success is organization. First, designate an area for your work. If possible, use a filing cabinet to store your materials, books, and assorted memorabilia. Next, you'll need several large, different colored looseleaf notebooks with pockets to store miscellaneous materials.

Use a separate notebook for each chapter activity (one for brainstorming, one for searching your family archives and treasures, etc.), and divide these notebooks into sub-sections using index tabs. These sub-sections will be used to store your two primary research forms: SOURCE DATA SHEETS and Q & A SHEETS, in addition to other miscellaneous papers and information.

Each chapter includes a list of suggested materials and resources which should help keep you organized.

Good organization also requires strong note-taking skills. Make it a habit to write legibly (a fine-point pen works best), use wide margins and spacing, and write on one side of the paper only. Be sure you always note your sources, dates, page numbers, and any other pertinent data on your SOURCE DATA SHEETS so you can easily refer back to your sources. This is particularly important if you're formally researching your line of descent to create your family tree as described in CHAPTER 8.

A tape recorder is another essential organizational tool if you choose to interview your relatives (CHAPTER 9). Be sure to note the date and type of information on the tapes before you store them, and to create some kind of coding system to make them easy to retrieve.

Optional tools and equipment include a camera and film, slide projector, small slide viewer, movie projector, video camera, video-cassette recorder, and art supplies. Use of these is explained in CHAPTER 10 - Incorporating Photography, Art, and Audio-Visual Equipment.

What are the basic procedures for researching my family's history and trivia?

Organize your information on SOURCE DATA SHEETS, use the Q & A SHEETS to work the information into questions and answers, choose your game's categories, and write your questions and answers on the Q & A CARDS.

What is a SOURCE DATA SHEET?

The purpose of the SOURCE DATA SHEET (Figure 1) is to systematically record all your information, no matter what your source. As you research, note your source and the source's date, and then write specific information from that source, including as many details as possible - because nearly every tidbit of information has the potential to become a question in your game.

For example, as Figure 2 indicates, we started with Aunt Grace's and Uncle Delen's 1946 diary, one of the volumes they kept for over fifty years. At first we were disappointed with these diaries because a typical entry consisted of a weather report and housecleaning details.

However, even though many entries didn't reveal any deep emotions, or juicy family tidbits, we were able to note lots of interesting information which later provided us with several questions. Much of the information noted in Figure 2 is directly related to our immediate family. "Bud" refers to our father, "Helen" is our maternal grandmother, the "two girls" are our mother and aunt, and "Claude" was our paternal grandfather. The point is: Don't give up no matter how insignificant the information may at first seem.

Also, don't reject a source because it appears too short to be helpful. Figure 2A is a brief letter our grandfather wrote to his sister shortly after Lorna's birth, and figure 2B is a corresponding SOURCE DATA SHEET example which demonstrates how simple it is to extract several bits of information from even a short letter. Because we knew we wanted to directly quote portions of this letter in our questions, we wrote some of this information as direct quotations. For the rest of the information, we noted the main ideas. Noting only the main ideas on the SOURCE DATA SHEET is faster and simpler than copying parts of your source word for word, but it's not quite as thorough and it may narrow your range of questions. You have to decide what's best for your purposes.

What is a Q & A SHEET?

The Q & A (Question and Answer) SHEET is designed so you can transfer your information to questions and answers before you write them on the Q & A CARDS, which are the question and answer cards for your game. CHAPTER 9: Writing The Game gives you more specific information on accomplishing this, but it's important to understand its basic function, and the choices you have regarding questions and categories.

Look again at Figure 2, first the completed SOURCE DATA SHEET, and then turn to Figure 4 which is a Q & A SHEET compiled from the information in Figure 2. You can see that the first question, "What kind of sandwich did Grace Bonsey eat on January 1, 1946, and why was that significant?", was written from the first bit of information on that SOURCE DATA SHEET.

And the next question, "According to the diary, how many times did Helen set pincurls in Elsie's hair in 1946?", resulted from looking at the overall picture. Had we bypassed the SOURCE DATA SHEET and chosen to use only the Q & A SHEET, we might have missed this fact. And even though the fact that Helen did Elsie's pincurls three times isn't a particularly significant family fact, it's amusing to us because these questions and answers offer insight into their personalities. Aunt Grace seldom ate fancy foods. Uncle Delen enjoyed women.

In terms of categories, the above question could fit into "Statistics", "Quotations", "Family Humor", "Names", or even "Miscellaneous". We would have missed all the possibilities of using these simple tidbits if we'd skipped the SOURCE DATA SHEETS and the Q & A SHEETS, and simply had written our questions while researching. This also holds true for Figure 4A, the QUESTION AND ANSWER SHEET example which is based on the letter our grandfather wrote to his sister. (See Figures 2A and 2B.) Notice the variety of both the questions and categories we were able to create from this one source! Follow our suggested procedures and you can do the same. And maybe along the way you, too, will discover some unexpected family history tidbits.

When can I begin?

Once you've organized your work area, gathered the necessary tools, made plenty of copies of the SOURCE DATA SHEETS and the Q & A SHEETS, and read this book so that you have a basic idea of the entire procedure, you're ready to embark on your family history and trivia search.

Keep an open, curious mind and approach your search as an adventure. Remember that you are the creator of your version of *IT'S ALL RELATIVE*; and that except for the game rules, there are no hard and fast regulations in this book.

The only requirement is to enjoy yourself as you reminisce about your family, research your roots, write the questions and answers, and share this very personalized game with your family.

Figure 1

SOURCE DATA SHEET

SOURCE: _____

CODE: _____

DATE: _____

INFORMATION:

Figure 2

SOURCE DATA SHEET EXAMPLE 1

SOURCE: Delen and Grace Bonsey's Diary

CODE: 9C

DATE: 1946

INFORMATION:

Jan. 1 -- "Had Italian sandwiches. I ate first one and liked it."

Jan. 14 -- "Delen put pincurls in Elsie's hair and mine."

Jan. 15 -- "Letter from Bud and pictures of his girl and him."

Jan. 19 -- "Delen made pincurls for me."

Jan. 25 -- "Delen made pincurls for Elsie."

Feb. 1 -- "Delen made pincurls for Elsie."

Feb. 11 -- "Delen made pincurls for me after supper."

June 16 -- "Got Delen and 2 girls and they rode to Bath with us. They had lunch then took bus to Freeport."

June 29 -- "Delen hadn't seen Junior for three years and I two years."

July 4 -- "The Bonseys had a family reunion today. 16 there in all. Harvey and Lettie, Aunt Anna, Claude, Rena, Olive, Junior, his family. Took snapshot of everyone."

July 18 -- "Had dinner at Claude's with Bud and his girl."

Nov. 22 -- "Delen got his first check tonight. He gets $1.20."

Dec. 6 -- "Gump and Earle moved into the living room for the winter."

11

Figure 2A

LETTER

STATE OF MAINE
State Liquor Commission
AUGUSTA

Dear Olive
          Lorna Jane 8-15-03
Arrived at 11 A.M. Aug 4
Every one fine. Helen is going
up today to stay with Osmond
until Ann comes home.
Sorry it isn't a boy but
them two girls will have
a lot of fun growing up
so close togeather
          Everything fine here
                    from Chuck

Figure 2B

SOURCE DATA SHEET EXAMPLE 2

SOURCE: Letter from Claude Bonsey to Olive Bonsey

CODE: 10A

DATE: May 1955

INFORMATION:

Lorna Jane weighed 8 lbs. 15 oz.

Lorna Jane born May 4 at 11:00 A.M.

"Helen is going to stay with Osmond until Ann comes home."

"Sorry it isn't a boy but the two girls will have a lot of fun growing up so close togeather [sic]."

State of Maine Liquor Commission letterhead

Figure 3

QUESTION AND ANSWER SHEET

QUESTION:

_____
_____
_____
_____

ANSWER:

_____
_____
_____
_____
_____
_____
_____

CODE:_____

CATEGORY: _____

Figure 4

QUESTION AND ANSWER SHEET EXAMPLE 1

QUESTION: What kind of sandwich did Grace Bonsey eat on Jan. 1, 1946, and why was that significant?
ANSWER: An Italian sandwich. First one she ever ate.
CODE: 9C
CATEGORY: Entertainment.

QUESTION: According to their diary, how many times did Delen set Elsie's hair in 1946?
ANSWER: Three.
CODE: 9C
CATEGORY: Statistics

QUESTION: Where did Delen and Grace take Helen and her two girls June 16, 1946?
ANSWER: Bath, Maine.
CODE: 9C
CATEGORY: Miscelleanous

QUESTION: In June 1946, how long had it been since Delen had seen Junior?
ANSWER: Three years.
CODE: 9C
CATEGORY: Statistics

QUESTION: Name three people who were at the Bonsey family reunion on July 4, 1946.
ANSWER: Any three of the following: Harvey, Lettie, Aunt Anna, Claude, Rena, Olive, Junior, and his family.
CODE: 9C
CATEGORY: Entertainment

QUESTION: What two people moved into Grace's and Delen's living room for the winter in December 1946?
ANSWER: Gump and Earle.
CODE: 9C
CATEGORY: Entertainment

15

Figure 4A

QUESTION AND ANSWER SHEET EXAMPLE 2

QUESTIONS: What was Lorna's birth weight?
ANSWER: 8 lbs. 15 ozs.
CODE: 10A
CATEGORY: Statistics

QUESTIONS: What is Lorna's middle name?
ANSWER: Jane
CODE: 10A
CATEGORY: Miscellaneous

QUESTIONS: What was Lorna's birthdate?
ANSWER: May 4, 1955
CODE: 10A
CATEGORY: Statistics

QUESTIONS: What time was Lorna born?
ANSWER: 11:00 A.M.
CODE: 10A
CATEGORY: Statistics

QUESTIONS: True or Flase - In a letter to Olive about Lorna's birth, Claude wrote, "Sorry it isn't a boy...."
ANSWER: True
CODE: 10A
CATEGORY: True or False

QUESTIONS: In a letter to Olive about Lorna's birth, which of the following words did Claude misspell? - arrived, Lorna, together
ANSWER: Together
CODE: 10A
CATEGORY: Entertainment

QUESTIONS: What letterhead stationary did Claude use when he wrote to Olive about Lorna's birth?
ANSWER: State of Maine Liquor Commission
CODE: 10A
CATEGORY: Miscellaneous

CHAPTER 3

Selecting Categories

This game is designed to allow you to select from four to eight categories. Select these categories on the basis of what fits your family: What activities do they participate in? Are they involved in the theatre?, Community Service?, Church? Is someone on a sports team? Is someone an automobile enthusiast? What are some family hobbies or pastimes?

We selected "Statistics", "Entertainment", "Sports", and "Miscellaneous" for our first version of *IT'S All RELATIVE*, and you'll find sample questions for each of these categories at the back of the book. These categories are so general that it wasn't difficult to assign questions to them. If you decide to use any of these four categories, the following summaries should prove useful.

Statistics

Answers for a statistics category are numerical. They can range from the obvious (dates, weights, amounts) to the obscure (telephone numbers, license plate numbers, blood types). Use the following hints and you'll be amazed at the number of questions you can write for this category.

Dates: Include birthdates, wedding dates, anniversary dates, graduation dates, dates of death, etc. Also include questions about dates or events that are important and unique to your family (baptisms, catechisms, bar mitzvahs)

Weights: Include birth weights, weight gains and losses, and write such questions as: How much weight did Aunt Jane gain during her first pregnancy? How much did Mom weigh when she was first married? How much did Lorna lose her first

19

week on Weight Watchers? How much would Lynn and Lorna like to weigh?

Prices: Research the cost of major purchases your family has made for such items as houses, automobiles, recreational vehicles, jewelry, boats, vacations, weddings, college. Give leeway on your questions: Within $2,000, how much did Mom and Dad pay for the camp? Include salary questions: How much did Gran earn per hour in her first job? How much per week did Dad get for his first raise?

How Many?: These questions are virtually endless and great fillers for categories that need help. Ask a question such as: How many fireplaces are in Ryan's house? Then substitute the word "fireplaces" with "windows", "doors", "telephones", or "bathrooms". Substitute "Ryan" with another relative's name. Substitute "house" with "living room" or "camp".

Entertainment

What does entertainment mean to your family?
To us it meant everything from dining out to school talent shows to Broadway plays. We also considered amusing incidents entertainment so we included such questions as: Where did Lynn go on her first date? and What was Cameron's role in the senior class talent show? and What play did the entire family see in New York City in 1985?
Other entertainment topics you might consider are movies, dating, vacations, parties, music, weddings, and birthdays.

Sports

Even though few members of our family ever participated in organized sports, we included a sports category. Our questions ranged from: What nickname did Lynn's gym teacher call her?, to: What was Cameron's best time in the 880 relay?
Sports to keep in mind if you select this category are swimming, hiking, canoeing, camping, fishing, race-car driving, boating, waterskiing, horseback riding, tennis, golf, basketball, racketball, gymnastics, and aerobics.
You may also want to refer to a sports chronology (see CHAPTER 2) to use statistics about a favorite sports team. Then you can include questions such as How many home runs did Hank Aaron hit the year Cameron was born? How old was

Dad when Babe Ruth was inducted into the Baseball Hall of Fame?

Miscellaneous

You may find that you have many excellent questions that just won't fit into a selected category. Or you may have several questions that would fit into a category, but wouldn't fill it.

If you include a "Miscellaneous" category in your game, you can use questions ranging from crazy: What celebrity does Bob resemble?, to off-beat: What Today Show host did Lorna meet in 1976?, to serious: Who was Lynn with when she heard Martin Luther King had been assassinated?, to challenging: How old was Mom when Dad became Town Manager of Yarmouth?

Your players will never know what to expect from this category!

Special notes

If you don't have enough questions to fill a category you really want to use, try combining it with another category. For instance – Fashion & Decades, Music & Decades, Food & Friends, Schools & Friends, Music & Special Occasions, Photographs & Quibbling Siblings.

Remember – your categories depend on your game's focus and your family's personality. We've designed the game to be flexible; you can use any of our category suggestions – or you can create your own categories. It's up to you.

List and Brief Descriptions of Possible Categories

Arts & Crafts:
Include Hobbies, Lessons, Gifts, Displays
Audio:
See CHAPTER 10
Awards & Trophies:
Sports, Professional, Clubs (Scouting, 4H), Dog/Horse Show Awards
Dates:
See page 13 and CHAPTER 5
Decades: Ask questions from the 20's, 30's, 40's, 50's, 60's, 70's' and 80's. If you're including an audio component, use songs from the decades. See CHAPTER 5 for further help.
Documents:
All the starred items in Figure 6, the FAMILY ARCHIVES INVENTORY
Entertainment:
See SAMPLE QUESTIONS
Family Tree:
See CHAPTER 8.
Fashion and Style:
Memorable Outfits, Jewelry, Car and House, Hair, Slang Expressions
Finances:
Debts, Prices, Banks, Loans, Lotteries, Gambling, Salaries
Food:
Diets, Likes & Dislikes, Restaurants, Picnics
Grab Bag:
See CHAPTER 10.
Health:
Maternity, Major Operations, Minor Irritations, Doctor Visits, Diet, Exercise
Miscellaneous:
See page 15 and SAMPLE QUESTIONS
Music:
Symphony, Recitals, Operas, Concerts, Special Occasions, Bands
Names:
Origins, Nicknames, Maiden Names, Surnames, Spelling
Oddities & Scandals:
Every family has them. Use your discretion.
Photographs: See CHAPTER 10

Quibbling Siblings:
Family Feuds, Silly Arguments.
Quotations:
Motherly Advice, Letter Excerpts, Misstatements, Baby's First Words/Sentences.
Schools:
Former Teachers, Classmates, Term Paper Topics, Courses, Report Cards, Gym Class, Activities, Dating.
Special Occasions:
Birthdays, Weddings, Showers, Christenings, Funerals.
Sports:
Physical Fitness, Athletics, Lessons. See page 14 and SAMPLE QUESTIONS.
Statistics:
See SAMPLE QUESTIONS.
Sweethearts:
Boyfriends, Girlfriends, Spouses, Ex-Loves.
Talents:
Music, Sewing, Singing, Dancing, Hobbies, Athletics.
Unique Relationships:
Volunteer work, Neighbors, Co-workers, Employers, The Public, Pets, Friends, Enemies, Relatives.

CHAPTER 4

Brainstorming

Getting started

Brainstorming is simply a matter of jotting down every-thing that comes into your mind about a subject. It's simple and fun - particularly when you're brainstorming information related to yourself. For this chapter, necessary materials in-clude a designated notebook, plenty of large scrap paper, writ-ing utensils, and several SOURCE DATA SHEETS. Optional materials include a clipboard, tape recorder, tapes, and any or all of the books which are mentioned in this chapter.

In all of this chapter's activities, you should jot your ideas down on scrap paper as quickly as you can. The next step is to transfer this information to your SOURCE DATA SHEETS, and from there you'll transfer the information to the Q & A SHEETS.

You do have the option of skipping the first step of jotting your thoughts down on scrap paper. However, we don't recom-mend it because during brainstorming it's important to "spill" your thoughts on paper without inhibition. If you record your initial thoughts on SOURCE DATA SHEETS and not on scrap paper, you may be overly-concerned with your handwriting or with keeping your thoughts in order, which will inhibit your spontaneity.

Brainstorming about you and your family experiences

When we started writing our family's game, we spent a hot summer day sunning ourselves on the dock at our Crescent Lake cottage in Raymond, Maine, the scene of countless won-derful summer memories. Pen and clipboard in hand, we jotted down trivia related to every memory we could recall:

Lynn's first kiss, Lorna's summer loves, escapades, boat rides, campfires, cook-outs, weird neighbors, funny relatives, and so on. One memory jogged another, and by the end of the day, sunburned and exhausted from laughing, we'd recalled a lot of family trivia.

We suggest that you start with this same brainstorming technique. Use blank scrap paper for your brainstorming sessions and don't worry about coherence, or even accuracy at this point. Just catch all those precious memories on paper.

To begin, think back to your earliest memory. Maybe it's a birthday party. Jot down everything you can recall about it. Where was it? When? Who were the guests? What was your favorite present? What were you wearing?

See how easy this is? You've already drawn a mental picture of that time by noting your memories. Granted, you won't necessarily use all these ideas for your game questions, but don't concern yourself with that. Just concentrate on reliving that moment in your life.

If you think of these events chronologically, you'll be less apt to forget important occurrences. Consider milestones, special activities, schools, addresses, friends, neighbors - anything at all related to you and your family.

If you are working with someone as you're brainstorming your memories, consider taping your conversation. Then you will have created a family legacy which can be transcribed into notes, or directly onto your SOURCE DATA SHEETS as suggested in the interview chapter.

When you note your information on a SOURCE DATA SHEET, your listed sources will be you and any people who helped you. You don't have to include everything that you've written on scrap paper or discussed on tape. You can edit your thoughts at this stage - or you can wait until you transfer the information to the Q and A SHEETS. What you include or leave out, and when you choose to do that will depend in large part on whether your game is focusing on current history, past history, or a combination of both.

Brainstorming about your relatives

When you've brainstormed all you can about yourself, do this same activity by concentrating on a family member, say your great-grandfather. Naturally, you'll have fewer ideas about him than you did yourself, unless he's alive or you're lucky enough to know a lot about him, but don't let that stop you. Consider physical features, emotional characteristics, irritating habits, favorite expressions, and so forth. Don't feel inhibited. Just list these on your scrap paper and again edit these thoughts later when you rework them onto the SOURCE DATA SHEETS or Q & A SHEETS for your game. For organizational purposes, use a separate sheet of scrap paper and SOURCE DATA SHEET for each relative.

Continue this brainstorming for as many members of your family as you can. Then move on to another brainstorming technique.

Word brainstorming

For this activity you simply use a word as a memory-starter. For instance, on scrap paper write an adjective as a heading as we've done below, and then list all the events, feelings, and comments, you can recall from that time.

EMBARRASSING: Lynn's missing falsie - Lorna's visit to the wrong party - Cameron's trip into a stranger's bathroom - Mom spilling wine on stranger - Dad driving wrong car

Later, when you fill out your SOURCE DATA SHEETS and your Q & A SHEETS, you can expand each of these moments by noting the story behind them, as in this example:

> WHO: Lynn and Rodney Saunders
> WHAT: Bra stuffed with falsie
> WHEN: 1968
> WHERE: Surry, Maine
> WHY: To impress Rodney with her "ample" figure

Or you can simply write a question such as: Who was Lynn trying to impress when she wore falsies on her first date?

Other possible words include: exciting, emotional, sentimental, frightening, sympathetic, conflict, affectionate, sensational, inspiring, thrilling, infuriating, passionate, frustrating, restless, peaceful, steady, panicked, patient, obedient, annoying glamourous, horrible, radiant, satisfying, remorse, celebration, humorous.

Thumb through any dictionary or thesaurus for further ideas.

Nostalgic brainstorming using places and objects

If possible, visit places which have some significance in your life: your childhood home, your grandparents' homes, vacation spots, schools, churches, etc. Bring along scrap paper and your clipboard – or better yet a tape recorder so you can record all of the many memories this brainstorming activity is apt to inspire. This activity is particularly valuable if you're writing the game with a family member. We spent some of our childhood in Freeport, Maine, home of L. L. Bean. Even though the town has grown and changed tremendously in the twenty-five years since we've lived there, a flood of memories still washes over us when we drive down Main Street, turn right, and pass our old house at 7 Chapel Street: lemonade stands, Bible School, Dad's flower gardens, Lynn's pretend wedding, a broken front tooth ... the list goes on and on. And every memory translates into at least one question.

If you're not interested, or simply unable to actually visit some places from your past, the next best thing is to walk down memory lane using your current environment.

Look around your living room. Anything catch your eye? How old is that painting? Where did Mom get that candlestick? Why is that knickknack cracked?

Now do the same with the other rooms and objects in your house. You'll be amazed at how easily your memories will flow.

Using books to brainstorm

With a little imagination and research, reference books and chronologies can add another dimension to your game. A chronology is a compilation of facts on a certain subject, listed in chronological order. For instance, if television has had an impact on your family, Rick Mitz's *The Great TV Sitcom Book*, a chronological synopsis of most of the television sitcoms from 1948 to 1979, should revive many happy moments of laughing at the antics of your favorite television characters.

The Complete Directory to Prime Time Network TV Shows by Tim Brooks and Earle Marsh is another excellent source for your game because it lists the following for each show: first and last telecasts, broadcast history, and the cast. It also includes the prime time schedules for 1948 to 1984.

These are especially useful because it's simple to find what shows were on then in a given year.

These television chronologies inspired the following questions and answers for our version of IT'S ALL RELATIVE:

What famous sitcom premiered the year Lorna was born? ("The Honeymooners", 1955)

In 1962, what show did Ann faithfully watch every Wednesday between 9:30 and 10:00 p.m.? ("The Dick Van Dyke Show")

What TV actor did Grambee insist was really crippled because of the part he portrayed? (Raymond Burr in "Ironside")

Why was one of Lynn's dates nicknamed Buddy? (He looked like Jack Sheldon who played Buddy on "Run Buddy Run".)

If there are movie buffs in your family, *The Great American Movie Book*, a reference guide to the best movies of the sound eras ranging from "Abbott and Costello Meet Frankenstein" to "Zorba the Greek", should also inspire plenty of family trivia ideas along the same lines:

How old was Kim the first time she saw "The Wizard of Oz"?

What did Lynn and Lorna sell to earn money to see "The Sound of Music"?

How many times did Pam see "Star Wars"?

Why did Mom get angry at Dad when they saw "Fatal Attraction"?

Also, if you choose to include an "audio" category (CHAPTER 10: Incorporating Photograhy, Art, and Audio-Visual Equipment), you could use portions of theme songs from favorite shows or movies, again by tying questions about them to your family members as in the upcoming examples. Such albums can frequently be found on discount racks at music stores. In their book, Brooks and Marsh include a list of some popular television theme songs.

In fact, you can do the same thing with other types of music - particularly rock and roll, which has affected almost everyone's lives in some way. *The Billboard Book of Number One Hits* by Fred Bronson lists over six hundred weekly number one hits for the years 1955–1985, and it also includes a brief description of each of these hits.

Sample questions and answers:

What was the number one song the week Cameron was born? ("The Battle of New Orleans", June 13, 1959)

At their wedding, what song did Lorna sing to John? ("Johnny Angel")

What was Lynn's favorite song from "The Sound of Music"?. ("My Favorite Things")

Should you include an audio component with your game, you'd play part of the song and rewrite the above questions:

This song was the number one hit the week Cameron was born. What's the title?

Why is this song significant to Lorna and John?

This is Lorna's favorite song from what movie?

Books related to hobbies and sports will also jar your memories. *The Way to Play: The Illustrated Encyclopedia of the Games of the World* is an example of this. It contains specific information on several different games. Just skimming through the book should remind you of games and related incidents of your childhood:

Which cousins were chess champions?

What did Lynn spill on the monopoly board?

During her senior year, what position did Lorna play on the girls' basketball team?

How much did Dad pay each of his children once they beat him at pingpong?

And even if your family, like ours, isn't particularly sports minded, with a little imagination, a book such as *The Encyclopedia of Sports* by Frank Menke will still prove valuable for brainstorming more family trivia. This comprehensive sports guide includes a tabulation of records and statistics, as well as historical highlights from many sports. To connect

30

this trivia with your family trivia, you can write questions such as:

Who won the world series the year Mom and Dad married? (1952 The New York Yankees)

Who won the Rose Bowl the year Mom was born? (1934 – Columbia)

Where were the Olympics held the year after Gran was born? (1912 Sweden)

Sure, some of these questions may seem far-fetched, but they'll add flavor and a sense of history to your game. Besides, your game will be more fun to play if it includes challenging questions.

Even a book such as a medical dictionary, which lists terms from "amnesia" to "wound", can give you ideas for both humorous and serious family trivia.

Every family has a funny tale to tell about someone suffering a temporary memory lapse, just as every family has been affected by injuries. Besides, including a family medical history component will add important information to your game.

Chronologies and compilations are also available on such diverse subjects as antiques, astrology, collectibles, cars, postcards, and photographs – many of which document the swift changes in our culture and history in the last century. Any of these books could prompt several more questions for your game.

Just continue to connect your family's trivia in any way possible. Remember: *It's All Relative.*

What's the next step?

It's up to you to decide your next step. If you've tried any or all of these brainstorming activities, you already have a wealth of family information. In fact, you may feel you have enough information to write your game. If so organize your information onto your SOURCE DATA SHEETS, and follow the directions in CHAPTER 11: Writing the Game.

However, if you want to continue your research, the following chapters will give you ideas for further researching your family history and writing your game.

CHAPTER 5

Connecting Historical Events to Your Family

Getting started

As Alex Haley clearly demonstrated in *Roots*, family heritage cannot be separated from history and culture. This chapter includes specific strategies and resources to connect historical events to your own roots - simply and quickly. If you use these strategies and resources, you'll gain a valuable perspective on your family's historical and cultural connections.

For this research activity, you need your designated notebook, several SOURCE DATA SHEETS, and the timeline we've included. Optional resources include history and reference books.

Using the timeline

The timeline includes significant United States historical events of the twentieth century. It also mentions several "firsts" which had an impact on our nation. It is *not* meant to be a comprehensive historical tool; rather it's intended to serve as a guideline of both significant and interesting events of the time - any of which could have affected your family.

There are two ways to use the timeline. One is to follow the suggested procedures for brainstorming as explained in CHAPTER 4. Another is to refer to it during your interviews (CHAPTER 9). Both of these activities will produce lots of information for your game.

For instance, if you are brainstorming about yourself, start with the first historical event you can recall. Jot down any information or feelings you have related to that time. For us, this meant starting in 1963, the year President Kennedy was assassinated. We noted where we were when we heard the news, our feelings and reactions, and our parents' reactions (from our perspective).

Later, when we interviewed them, we asked them specific questions related to this horrible event. From this one event, we added over twenty questions to our game.

Another strategy you can use is to connect historical events to your family by asking "trick" questions which may require a knowledge of history or some mathematical calculations. For example:

What were the combined ages of Lynn, Lorna, and Cameron in the year President Kennedy was assassinated?

When Michael was born, who was president?

How many presidents have there been during Ryan's lifetime?

How old was Grambee when Prohibition began?

What was the first year Cameron voted?

In 1972, whom did Lynn cast her presidential vote for?

What famous criminal was shot by the FBI the year Mom was born?

Use your imagination and this timeline and you can develop literally hundreds of questions and answers which connect your family to history.

Genealogy how-to books, history books, and compilations of historical facts will further assist you should you want more in-depth information.

We used both *The Encyclopedia of American Facts and Dates* and *The People's Chronology: A Year-by-Year Record of Human Events From Prehistory to the Present* as sources for the timeline. If you want your game to contain more of a historical and/or cultural perspective, each of these chronologies contains countless historical facts which you can combine with your family history to create an outstanding family keepsake.

TIMELINE

1900 –

McKinley Elected President – Brownie Box Camera Introduced by Kodak – Texas Hurricane Kills Thousands

1901 –

McKinley Assassinated – Theodore Roosevelt Sworn In As President

1902 –

Teddy Bear Introduced in U.S.

1903 –

Roosevelt Orders warships to Panama – Fire Kills Hundreds in Chicago Theatre – First Pacific Cable Opens – First Successful Wright Brothers' Flight – Ford Motor Company Begins

1904 –

Roosevelt Elected President – New York City Subway Opens – World Series Cancelled

1905 –

Yellow Fever Epidemic in New Orleans

1906 –

Earthquake Destroys San Francisco

1907 –

Oklahoma Admitted to the Union – First Self-Contained Electric Washing Machine

1908 –

Taft Elected President – Model T Introduced – U.S. Banks Close – Robert Peary First Man To Reach North Pole – First Observance of Mother's Day

1909 –

Lincoln Penny Replaces Indian Head

1910 –

Several States Adopt Prohibition – Halley's Comet Passes The Sun – Boy Scouts of America Founded – First Observance of Father's Day

1911 –

Mexico and Arizona Admitted to the Union

1912 –

Roosevelt Shot – Woodrow Wilson Sworn In As President – Titanic Sinks – Girl Scouts of America Founded

1913 –

Federal Reserve System Established

1914 –

Outbreak of World War I – Panama Canal Opens

1916 –

Wilson Re-elected President

1917 –

U. S. Declares War Against Germany

1918 –

First Airmail Service – Influenza Epidemic – Germany Surrenders

1919 –

Prohibition

1920 –

"Roaring Twenties" Begin – Harding Elected President

1921 –

Ku Klux Klan Causes Violent Incidents – U.S. Signs Peace Treaty With Germany

1922 –

Women's Suffrage Amendment Declared Constitutional

1923 –

President Harding Dies – Coolidge Sworn In As President

1924 –

Midwest Tornado Worst In U.S. History

1925 –

Charleston Popular Dance – Scopes Trial

1926 –

"Permanent" Zipper Invented

1927 –

First Solo Nonstop Flight From New York to Paris by Charles A. Lindbergh – Transatlantic Telephone Service Begins – First Full Length Talking Picture

1928 –

Herbert Hoover Elected President

1929 –

Stock Market Crash – 16mm Home Movie Camera Introduced

1931 –

Clairol Hair Dye Introduced

1932 –

President Hoover Orders Five Day Work Week To Be Standard – Franklin Roosevelt Elected President – Charles A. Lindbergh Jr. Kidnapped – Amelia Earhart First Woman to Solo Across Atlantic – New Deal Introduced By Roosevelt

1933 –

Repeal of Prohibition – Banks Begin To Reopen – Hitler Becomes Dictator of Third Reich

1934 –

John Dillinger Shot By FBI – Dionne Quintuplets Born

1935 –

Roosevelt Signs Social Security Act – Huey Long Shot To Death

1936 –

Roosevelt Re-elected

1937 –

Amelia Earheart Disappears – Hindenburg Explodes

1938 –

Hurricane kills hundreds in New England

1939 –

World Fairs in New York and San Francisco

1840 –

Nylon Stockings First Go On Sale – Franklin Roosevelt Re-elected president

1941 –

Pearl Harbor Attacked by Japan – U.S. Declares War Against Germany and Italy

1942 –

Tokyo Bombed by U.S. – Coffee, Sugar, Gas Rationing

1943 –

Widespread Race Riots – Infantile Paralysis Epidemic

1944 –

D-Day – Franklin Roosevelt Re-elected President

1945 –

Franklin Roosevelt Dies – Harry Truman Sworn In As President – United Nations Starts – Japan and Germany Surrender – Hiroshima Attacked By First Atomic Bomb

1946 –

Spiraling Inflation

1947 –

Jackie Robinson First Black Baseball Player

1948 –

Harry Truman Elected President

1949 –

Alger Hiss Trial

1950 –

President Truman Orders Forces to So. Korea – President Truman Declares State of National Emergency

1951 –

Japanese Peace Treaty Signed

1952 –

Dwight Eisenhower Elected President

1953 –

Rosenberg Trial

1954 –

McCarthy Investigations

1955 –

Racial Segregation in Schools Banned

1956 –

Salk Anti-polio Vaccine Available – Eisenhower Re-elected

1957 –

Sputnik I Launched By Soviets – Forced Integration Causes Racial Violence

1958 –

Serious Recession – Alaska and Hawaii Become States

1959 –

Premier Krushchev Visits U.S.

1960 –

U. S. U-2 Plane Shot Down In U.S.S.R. – John F. Kennedy Elected President

1961 –

School Integration Marked By Sporadic Violence

1962 –

Cuban Missile Crisis – Three U. S. Astronauts Orbit The Earth

1963 –

President Kennedy Assassinated – Lyndon B. Johnson sworn in as President – Submarine "Thresher" Lost in Atlantic – Medgar Evans Murdered

1964 –

Civil Rights Act Enacted – New York World's Fair – Johnson Elected President

1965 –

Vietnam Protests Increase – First U.S. Walk in Space – New York City Blackout

1966 –

Vietnam War Escalates – Worst Blizzard in 70 Years in East

1967 –

Worst Race Riots in Nation's History – Three Astronauts Killed at Cape Kennedy – Muhammed Ali Sentenced for Refusal To Be Drafted

1968 –

President Johnson Doesn't Seek Re-election – Martin Luther King Assassinated – Robert Kennedy Assassinated – Violence Marks Democratic Convention – Richard Nixon Elected President

1969 –

First Artificial Heart Implant – First Moon Landing – Draft Lottery Becomes Law

1970 –

Cigarette Ads Banned on TV and Radio – Kent State Riots – Earth Day Observed

1971 –

Massive Bombardment of Vietnam – Voting Age Lowered to 18

1972 –

President Nixon Visits China and Moscow – George Wallace Shot – Discovery of Watergate Break-In – Nixon Re-elected in Landslide

1973 –

Vietnam Peace Agreement Signed – Supreme Court Rules for Abortion – Watergate Committee Hearings – Vice President Agnew Resigns

1974 –

President Nixon Resigns – Gerald Ford Sworn in As President

1975 –

Vietnam War Ends

1976 –

Jimmy Carter Elected President – Patty Hearst Convicted of Bank Robbery

1977 –

Draft Resisters Pardoned

1978 –

Casino Gambling Opens In Atlantic City

1979 –

Three Mile Island Near Nuclear Disaster – U.S. Embassy in Teheran Seized

1980 –

Mt. St. Helens Erupts – Ronald Reagan Elected President

1981 –

Reagan Shot by John Hinckley – Sandra Day O'Connor First Woman on Supreme Court

1982 –

Cyanide Planted In Tylenol Capsules

1983 –

Beirut Embassy Bombed – Sally Ride Becomes First Woman in Space

1984 –

Geraldine Ferraro Becomes First Woman Presidential Running Mate

1985 –

Achille Lauro Hijacked

1986 –

U. S. Strike Against Libya – First Surrogate Birth of Test Tube Baby

1987 –

Iran Contra Hearings – PTL Scandal

CHAPTER 6

Searching Your Family Archives For Treasures And Trivia

Getting started

Because we've always saved and savored our family memorabilia, our attics and closets are filled with letters, cards, notes, calendars, journals, diaries, home movies, photographs, family records, and assorted other treasures. As a result of our family "treasure" hunt, we created some of our best questions. In this chapter, we'll show you how to do the same.

First, make a copy of FAMILY ARCHIVES INVENTORY (figure 6). If you make a hand-written copy, be sure to include the four headings: "Number", "Records", "Location", "Progress Notes", and to leave plenty of space between each item.

Once you've done this, use a pencil to fill in your known available items under each major category, their locations, and any special notes. The purpose of the "Progress Notes" section is to keep you organized while allowing you to check your progress at a glance.

Now look at Figure 7 which is a completed section of a FAMILY ARCHIVES INVENTORY sheet. A quick glance tells you that three of these records have been completely researched, which means their information has been noted on SOURCE DATA SHEETS. Record 9C, Delen's and Grace's fifty-two year diaries have been partially researched, and record 9B, Osmond Bonsey's diaries, are not completely researched and we need permission to use selected pages.

When possible, include the dates of any of your records or mementos. (Dating them not only ensures accuracy – it provides a quick reference should you to decide to use "Dates" as one of your game categories.)

When you've completed your inventory as much as possible on your own, you may want to write to family members to check on the availability of certain items. If you do this, enclose a copy of your inventory so they can see both what you have, and what you might need. Consider doing this in round-robin fashion so that the same inventory form is passed from relative to relative, rather than sending separate forms and letters. This procedure may jar someone's memory and provide unexpected family trivia records and information.

Also, don't be surprised or hurt if someone is reluctant to loan you a family memento. As in the case of our father's diaries mentioned above (Osmond Bonsey), he was willing to share certain information from his diaries, but he certainly wasn't going to allow us to read every page of his personal thoughts - which is understandable.

After you've determined the location of most of the records you intend to use, cross out each category you don't intend to use. Then use the first column on the FAMILY ARCHIVES INVENTORY to number each major category you will be using. It's likely you'll have more than one record under each category so assign a letter to each of those records also (9A, 9B, 9C, 9D, and 9E in Figure 7). Duplicate enough SOURCE DATA SHEETS so that you have at least one for each record.

Using tab dividers, organize your notebook for this chapter into sections, one for each record. As you complete your SOURCE DATA SHEETS, insert them in these sections for easy reference.

Retrieving information

Now the real fun begins: Retrieving information from your family records and mementos.

The amount of family trivia you can find will depend on the type of memorabilia you're researching, but the basic procedure is the same: Use your imagination and note every possible tidbit related to that item on the SOURCE DATA SHEET. For a good example of this, refer to CHAPTER 2, Figures 2, 2A, 2B, 4, and 4A, where we demonstrated step-by-step how tidbits of information from our aunt's and uncle's diary, and our grandfather's letter became interesting trivia questions.

Diaries and journals are probably the easiest family mementos to pull information from. However, with practice and persistence, you can use pieces of information from every family memento.

Report cards are a good example of this. You can get at least fifty questions from each report card. For instance, figure 5 is our father's report card for the third and fourth periods of the school year 1937-1938 when he was in the fourth grade. There are thirty-four ranks on this page alone, and each one of those has the potential to be a question. (During the third period of fourth grade, what rank did Osmond receive in reading? arithmetic? composition? ....)

If you have a "Statistics" category, you could ask questions such as: How many A's did Osmond receive on his report card in fourth grade? Or, how many days was Osmond absent from school during the fourth period of fourth grade?

If you have other family member report cards for the same grades, you could also write comparison questions: In third grade, who received more A's - Ann, Osmond, or Cameron? Or, in third grade, who was absent the most?

Letters are also invaluable sources of information about your family. They can provide innumerable questions and reveal clues to personalities, relationships, and situations. For example, each of the following quotations, which were written twenty-six years apart by two different fathers to their sons, gives just such clues:

"It gives me a good feeling when I think of the responsible position my son has, but I'm sure he can handle it o.k."

"I am proud of you as a son who's liked and respected by so many people."

These quotes are examples of the caring relationships these fathers and sons shared, (the first quote is from our paternal grandfather to our father; the second from our father to our brother), and this information can by used in your game by asking players to identify the speaker, the son, the situation, and maybe even the date of these quotes.

These are just two sentences from entire letters which are filled with useable information.

(Of course, you need to use your discretion when quoting from family letters. To be sure the information you're using won't offend anyone, it's probably best to get permission before quoting from a letter. After all, you don't want your family history game to become "Family Feud".)

Letters from people other than family members can also prove interesting and provide more clues as in these examples:

"April 6, 1949

Dear Mr. Bonsey,
In a letter just received from Elmer Kane, regarding tax matters, I have learned of your illness and have asked Mr. Kane to personally express my good wishes to you.
During the long years of my acquaintanceship with you, with periodic lapses, I have always regarded you as a typical example of Maine manhood and fine character ..."

This letter was written to our paternal Great-Grandfather by a gentleman from New York City who "summered" near him. It gives clues to how others viewed him, as well as to his illness - clues we used in our game.

"November 16, 1969

Dear Mr. and Mrs. Bonsey,
I really hated to give Lynn the D in Algebra and I also know she was almost broken-hearted to receive it. I know she can do much better work and that her grade will be greatly improved at the half year mark. Lynn is a fine girl and it is a pleasure to have her in my class."

This letter was written by Lynn's algebra teacher. Possible questions include:
Fill in the missing word in the following letter quote: "I really hated to give _____ the D in Algebra. OR - "I really hated to give Lynn the _____ in _____. OR - In what year did Lynn receive a D in algebra? OR - What teacher wrote Mom and Dad a note apologizing for giving Lynn a bad grade?
You should realize by now that your family archives may be filled with trivia. It's just a matter of finding and sorting through this memorabilia. To help you, we've included individual "hints" for retrieving information from each of the categories in the FAMILY ARCHIVES INVENTORY. It's a given that you should note names and dates for each of these categories. The words "pictures" or "artwork" refer to CHAPTER 10: Incorporating Photography, Art, And Audio-Visual Equipment which describes how you can use pictures and artwork to create questions for these categories.
As you use these hints, keep in mind that no detail is too trivial for your family history game!

44

(The starred records are also considered to be primary sources. CHAPTER 7 provides further information about researching and using them.)

Address Books: complete addresses, number and street addresses, towns/cities lived in, number of moves, zip codes

Autograph Books: signers names, signature dates, number of signatures, famous people, copies of signatures for game players to identify

*Baby Books: gift-givers and types of gifts, baby's full name and statistics (birth weight, height, date, time), "firsts"

*Baptism/Christening Papers: date, faith, child's age, church, minister/priest/rabbi

*Bibles/Book Inscriptions: book's original owner, handwritten entries (copy and identify or quote from), dates, signatures

*Birth Certificates: name, parents' names, place of birth, date

*Bonds, Mortgages, Deeds: names, dates, loan & interest amounts, collateral, terms and conditions, land descriptions, witnesses, locations

Coats of Arms: colors, crest, helmet, wreath, mantle, shield, motto, origins

Collections: origins, owners, numbers, worth, types, pictures, artwork

*Contracts/Leases: dates, amounts, stipulations, parties involved

*Death Certificates: names, dates, causes, places

*Diaries/Journals/Logs: dates, events, feelings, direct quotations, comparisons of two different entries, anecdotes, copies

Employment Records: names, work length, salary, benefits, sick days, raises, positions, supervisors

Family Histories/Genealogies: author(s), family tree

*Financial Records: names, amount, due date, interest

*Gravestones: birthdates, death dates, survivors, epitaphs, pictures of rubbings, locations, etchings, artwork

*Health Records: names, hospitalizations, diseases, dates, hospital names, doctors

Household Items: origins, furniture, knick-knacks, books, paintings, antiques, worth, pictures, artwork

Jewelry: worth, location, owners, antiques, significance, types of metal and stones, carat, weight, size, pictures, artwork

*Ledgers: prices, items, store/company names, product lists, totals

*Letters/Notes/Postcards: quotations, postmarks, signatures, copies, greetings/closings, unusual language, handwriting

*Licenses: purpose, signatures, issue and expiration dates, terms and conditions, mottos, insignias

Maps: locations, area, distances

*Marriage Certificates: names, date, attendants, officiator, signatures, ages

*Membership Records: organizations, membership dates, offices held, locations

*Military Records/Medals: names, ranks, inscriptions, locations

Newspaper Clippings: paper, name, who, what, when, where, why

*Passports: places travelled, expiration dates, ages, number of "stamps"

Photographs, Slides, Movies, Videos: See CHAPTER 10

Prizes: trophies/models/ribbons/pins/certificates: dates, inscriptions, pictures, artwork, signatures, reasons

*Report Cards/Transcripts: grades, behavior, comments, teachers, promotions, comparisons, absences, tardies

Scrapbooks/Souvenirs: dates, names, locations, numbers (how many birthday cards? pictures? ticket stubs?)

Tapes: (Reel-to-reel, cassette): See CHAPTER 10

*Wills: executor, names, dates, stipulations, bequeathals, witnesses, types

Yearbooks: superlatives, pictures, class song, autographs

Miscellaneous: Use your imagination!

Figure 5

REPORT CARD 1938

THIRD PERIOD ....6....Weeks		FOURTH PERIOD ....6....Weeks	
The average rank for this period is———		The average rank for this period is———	
A means 90-100% Unusually Successful Work		A means 90-100% Unusually Successful Work	
B means 80- 89% Very Successful Work		B means 80- 89% Very Successful Work	
C means 70- 79% Average Work		C means 70- 79% Average Work	
D means 60- 69% Below Average Work		D means 60- 69% Below Average Work	
E means 0- 59% Unsuccessful Work		E means 0- 59% Unsuccessful Work	
The passing grade is———		The passing grade is———	
Reading ....B	Physiology ....B	Reading ....B	Physiology ....B
Arithmetic ....B	Health Habits ....—	Arithmetic ....B	Health Habits ....—
English:	Science ....—	English:	Science ....—
Composition ....B-	Music C	Composition ....B	Music C
Grammar ....B	Drawing ....A-	Grammar ....B	Drawing ....B
Oral ....B	Projects ....—	Oral ....B	Projects ....—
Spelling ....B+	Use of Library ....—	Spelling ....B+	Use of Library ....A
Penmanship ....B	Arts and Crafts ....—	Penmanship ....B	Arts and Crafts ....—
History ....A	Domestic Science ....—	History ....B	Domestic Science ....—
Geography ....B		Geography ....B	
Civics ....—		Civics ....B	
Sportsmanship ....B-	Initiative ....B	Sportsmanship ....B-	Initiative ....B
Effort ....B	Courtesy ....B+	Effort ....B	Courtesy ....B
Days Absent 8	Days Tardy ....—	Days Absent 5½	Days Tardy ....—
Signed *Hilda Allen*		Signed *Hilda Allen*	
TEACHER		TEACHER	
Signed *Rena Bailey*		Signed *Rena Bailey*	
PARENT		PARENT	

47

Figure 6

FAMILY ARCHIVES INVENTORY

No.	Record Type	Location	Progress

Figure 7

FAMILY ARCHIVES INVENTORY EXAMPLE

No.	Record	Location	Progress
9	Diaries/Journals/Logs		
	A. Lynn Bonsey 1968–1988	Lynn's House	Completely Researched
	B. Osmond Bonsey 1977–1988	Dad's House	Can use only selected pages. See Dad.
	C. Delen/Grace Bonsey 1927–1975	Lynn's House	Completely Researched 1927–1946; Need to research 1947–1975
	D. Sofia Andulsia Winchester 1871	Lynn's House	Completely Researched
	E. Augusta Bunker 1883	Lynn's House	Haven't Used Yet
10	**A.** Claude's Letter to Olive 4 May 1955	Lorna's House	Completely Researched
	B. Brandon's Postcard to Michael May 18, 1986	Kim's House	Haven't Used Yet

CHAPTER 7

Searching Public Records For Family Information

Researching the primary and secondary sources related to your family will be the most time-consuming aspect of creating *IT'S ALL RELATIVE*. However, don't let this stop you from pursuing family information. Remember, it isn't necessary to complete all your research before you first play your game.

If you intend to focus your game on your current family, and you're not interested in including a formal or genealogical component, then it's not necessary for you to refer to this chapter.

However, if you do want to learn more about your ancestors' lives, researching the following records will help you verify what you already know about your family, discover new information and maybe even disclaim some family legends. The following information is merely an introduction to tracking down these records. The bibliography includes several books you'll find useful should you decide to learn more about genealogy and to extensively trace your roots.

Libraries

Libraries contain a wealth of useful information for tracing your roots, but the amount and type of information vary greatly from one library to another. For instance, the Library of Congress in Washington, D.C., provides references to family genealogists but does not undertake research on family histories. However, you can use its local history and general reading room where there are 10,000 indexes and guides available for your perusal. Then there's the Genealogical Society of the Church of Latter-Day Saints which contains the largest genealogical collection of documents in the world with more than one million rolls of microfilm covering vital statistics, church, cemetery, probate, and land records for millions of people. Several of its branch libraries are located throughout the United States.

Although these two libraries contain immense information, don't be discouraged if you don't have access to them. They do offer limited reference services through the mail, but if you're not sure what you're looking for, it's wise to start by concentrating your efforts on the libraries closest to your ancestors' localities. Sources to research include: atlases and local maps - county histories - town/city reports, town/city records - town/city/state directories - telephone directories - reference books (almanacs, encyclopedias) - published genealogies - miscellaneous books - bibliographical indexes - vital statistics - newspapers - census records.

Any of these sources may contain clues to your family history as we discovered when we searched through the *Maine Register* a state yearbook published annually since 1822. It contains, among other things, a calendar, postage rates, state boards, court directory, churches, businesses, and county and town statistics. The 1960 volume was fascinating because in his capacity as Freeport town manager, our father's name and the names of several people we knew were listed. And under the town of Surry, Maine, our parents' hometown, we discovered our maternal grandfather's name listed twice - as a painter and as a superintendent of a local cemetery. It was fun to see these names in print because these were real people to us. If you use some of these resources, some of your ancestors may become real to you, too.

Before you go to the library you need to determine your goals. Are you looking for historical information? Searching for specific information related to your family? Or not sure what you'll find?

Whatever your goals and whatever the library, you should familiarize yourself with the books and documents available, and learn the procedures for using the card catalog and microfilm machines before you attempt to do anything else. Many libraries house genealogical collections in a separate section where most librarians will be more than willing to assist you. Try to be specific and reasonable in your requests. In other words, don't expect the librarian to do your research for you; the librarian's role is to lead you to the needed sources. Your role is to research those sources.

National Archives

The National Archives, located in Washington, D.C., also contains millions of records which are useful for genealogical research. Most of the records can be examined by the general public at the National Archives or at its eleven field branches throughout the United States. The completeness of these records varies from full to very little information.

The following types of records are stored in the National Archives:

Census Schedules: Every ten years since 1790 (except for most of the 1890 schedule which was destroyed by fire). All of these schedules are available on microfilm.

Mortality Schedules: Available from the 1850-1880 censuses from some states.

Indian Records: Cover 1830-1940

Federal Land Records: Mainly from 1800-1974

Naturalization Records: All United States Naturalizations after September 26, 1906. From 1802 - 1906 the Naturalization Proceedings of the District of Columbia courts only.

Passenger Lists: Several incomplete lists ranging from 1820-1854

Passport Applications: 1791-1926

Personnel Records: Limited amount of information on civilian employees

Military Records: extensive - covering all branches.

For further information, write to the National Archives and Records Administration in Washington, D.C., 7th and Pennsylvania Avenue NW, Washington DC 20408, and ask for the pamphlets *Using Records in the National Archives for Genealogical Research* and *Military Service Records in the National Archives of the United States.*

In terms of state, county, and local records, historical societies are also good places to start your research. Frequently they house valuable, rare documents about an area. Sometimes they include local records, published histories, and other sources as listed under "Libraries" at the beginning of this chapter.

State, county, and local records

Unfortunately, standard procedures for collecting data from state to state and even from county to county or town to town do not exist. Consequently, you have to proceed accordingly depending on the area you're searching and the information you're researching. Following is a brief list of important records and thier possible locations. (Should you wish to do extensive research, the bibliography in the back of this book lists several books which explain these records and their locations in much greater detail.)

Land Records (mortgages, deeds, leases, contracts): Generally found in county courts. Exist from first permanent settlements. Contain significant data on land transactions between individuals.

Vital Statistics (birth, marriage, death): Generally found in county courts, but may also be found in state or local records.

Probate Records (wills, inventories, beneficiaries, guardianships): Generally found in county courts.

Civil Suits (divorce, custody disputes, foreclosures): Generally found in count courts.

Cemetery Records (usually include vital statistics): Generally found in town where cemetery is located. If a church cemetery, the church or historical society may have the records.

Church Records: Generally kept by the church.

Miscellaneous Records (tax, voter registration, maps, membership rolls): Generally kept by the town.

Searching for your roots can be a long process. There are countless records and documents to investigate, many facts to keep track of, and all of this takes lots of time. However, if you get to the point where you hit a roadblock or you feel overwhelmed, don't get discouraged. Just keep in mind that every single piece of information and every tidbit of trivia you accumulate is actually a piece of you, your family, and your future generations.

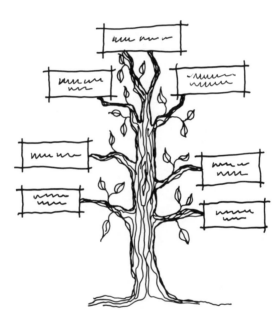

CHAPTER 8

Creating And Including Your Family Tree

Creating your family tree and including its information in your game may require some of the research detailed in the previous chapter on searching public records, or it may simply involve interviewing your relatives and/or sorting through memorabilia. It depends on how much information you start with, and how far back you'd like to trace your ancestors.

Generally a family tree, or pedigree, is defined as a line of descent which starts with you and "branches" out to include as many ancestors as possible. Professional genealogists spend a considerable amount of time researching and compiling that data by using several types of systematic detailed coding charts. If your goal is to write a comprehensive family history and to extensively research your pedigree then you should consult some of the books listed in the bibliography. If your goal is to create a basic, direct descendancy pedigree chart as shown in figure 8, you can do that by finding the pertinent information and then following these directions.

Using figure 8, start with yourself by writing your full name on the line following "1". (Do not use abbreviations. Nicknames should be written in parentheses after the full name.)

Under your name fill in the pertinent vital statistics. The abbreviations represent: birthdate and place; marriage date and place, death date and place, and burial place. Dates should be written with the day first, then the month and year (17 March 1905).

Once you've filled in the pertinent information about yourself, you've formed the "trunk" of your family tree.

On line two, write your father's name and accompanying information. Write your mother's name and her vital statistics on line three. List your father's mother and father on lines four and five; your mother's parents on lines six and seven, your father's grandparents, your father's paternal grandparents on lines eight and nine; your father's maternal grandparents on lines ten and eleven, your mother's paternal grandparents on lines twelve and thirteen, and your mother's maternal grandparents on lines fourteen and fifteen.

For easy reference and consistency always list the men on the even numbers and the women as odd numbers. If you do this, the father's number will always be twice the number of his children and his wife's number will always be one less than her husband's.

Once you've filled in as many names and vital statistics as possible, you will have completed a four-generation chart. This single chart can give you one hundred questions for your game by using a combination of the names and vital statistics: - Who was ?'s paternal grandfather? - What was ?'s middle name? - What were the first names of ?'s paternal great-grandparents? - How many years separated ?'s and ?'s deaths? - Where is ? buried? - Of ?, ?, and ?, who was the oldest when he died?, when he married?

You can easily substitute other names for the above to get your hundred questions.

If you are lucky enough or persistent enough to have information to trace your family tree back more than four generations, then you can either continue the chart by drawing your own, or you can purchase one at a historical society or store specializing in genealogical research. (Each fourth generation will be repeated as the first generation on the next chart.)

Should you decide that you want to include more than just "direct" ancestors, you'll want to include family group charts.

A family group chart (or record) focuses on one member from the pedigree chart. Its purpose is to include more details about that one person, many of which do not appear on the pedigree chart: other spouses names, childrens' names and the dates and places of their births and deaths, occupation, and religion.

Family group charts are vital to genealogists because, like the pedigree chart, they contain lots of information at a glance. However, neither the pedigree chart or family group chart is a "standard" genealogical form. These forms vary from book to book. Again, you can buy these sheets from a bookstore specializing in this type of research, or you can refer to several of the genealogy books listed in the bibliography which contain pedigree and family group charts.

For easy reference be sure to "code" the family group sheets to correspond to the numbers on your pedigree chart.

The further you continue your search backwards, the more difficult it will be to find information for your pedigree chart and family group sheets, but don't let this disoourage you. Be persistent, take your time, and remember that whatever information you compile, no matter how limited it may be, will strengthen your personal connection to the past.

Each piece of this information can become a question and answer for your game – and who knows – maybe a family member can help you fill in some of those missing tidbits while you're playing *IT'S ALL RELATIVE*!

Figure 8

PEDIGREE CHART

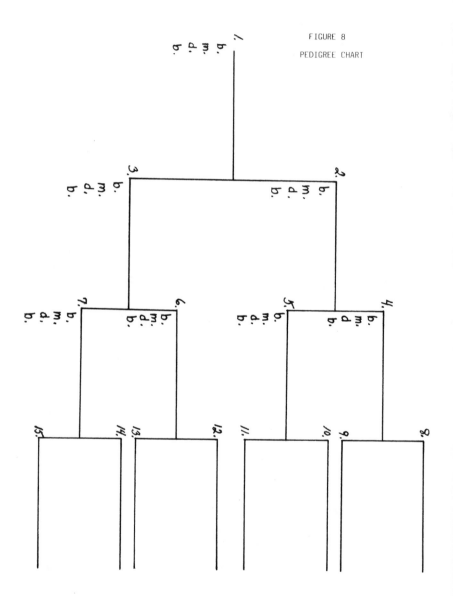

FIGURE 8

PEDIGREE CHART

60

CHAPTER 9

Interviewing

Interviewing is a good way to get information without having to do a lot of research. In this chapter, we explain how to conduct various types of interviews so that you can maximize the number of questions for your game.

Informal interviews

When you think about it, every conversation is an informal interview. If you are writing this game secretly to give as a surprise gift, and you find you need specific information from the person for whom you're writing the game, use the informal interview approach. Conversation starters such as "Remember when ...?" should initiate several stories with details you can use in your game. And a simple comment or question may remind the person of something which makes him/her reveal a lot of valuable information.

Make "mental" notes until you are able to write them down. In fact, if you're like us, as you get further into researching and writing your game, you'll find that you'll be mentally taking notes and forming questions during most of your conversations with family members.

Formal interviews

When your interviewee is aware that he/she is being interviewed, follow these steps:

Prior to the interview give the person an idea of the subject(s) you intend to cover. You can do this orally or in a letter.

Have your questions prepared in advance and write the answers as you conduct the interview. That way, you'll be able to refer to the answers easily when you transfer all of it to the SOURCE DATA SHEETS.

Use a video camera or tape recorder if you have one available. Once the interviewee forgets that the equipment is in the room, he or she will be relaxed and spontaneous since you won't be constantly interrupting with, "Wait a minute. I want to write that down."

Our grandmother was hesitant about being recorded, but when she finally relaxed and forgot about the tape recorder, the planned thirty minute interview turned into an hour and a half, and she didn't want to stop talking when the tape ran out! That interview contains priceless family information from her perspective, and she even revealed feelings and facts she'd never told anyone before.

If you do decide to videotape your interviews, *Video Family Portraits* by Ron Huberman and Laura Janis contains guidelines for operating the equipment, and conducting the interviews.

If you intend to incorporate photographs into your game, show pictures during the video or audio taping, and have the person respond to them. Then you'll be able to include questions and answers related to these responses. (See CHAPTER 10 for more details.)

If you have recorded an interview, you have two choices. Transcribe the interview word-for-word, or listen to the tape and jot down only the important, relevant portions.

We suggest transcribing the tape word-for-word. Even though transcribing is time consuming and tedious, this procedure will give you more details for your questions than if you don't write everything down.

An example of a word-for-word transcription follows. This is a portion of a tape-recorded interview with our maternal grandmother.

"Aunt May was the oldest and was a half sister to my mother and she married a Mosher and he was a cooper in Boothbay and they had a big house, bay window, beautiful view. Have to go on a footbridge to go to their house. Her husband died many years before she did. When we lived in Freeport, Grace and Delen went with us and we went there and she had a sandwich with us and she was showing us the house and she was so pleased with that house. She was a little woman who wore a pug and she had long black skirts that went down to the ankle. She was what I call a cute, little old lady, just as bright as she can be. Going through that house while she was there, Delen said, 'Isn't that a nice place for a casket?' I almost went into hysterics."

Some of the questions we wrote from this very short piece are as follows: - How was Aunt May related to Gran's mother? - What was Aunt May's married name? - Where did Aunt May live? - What was Aunt May's husband's occupation? - What did you cross to get to Aunt May's house -- a footbridge, railroad tracks, or a stone wall? - How did Aunt May wear her hair? - What was the length of Aunt May's skirts?

Chances are if we hadn't transcribed this piece word for word, we would have missed several potential questions. Granted, some of these questions may seem insignificant, but remember, this is a trivia game. Any and all questions apply.

If you don't have the time or inclination to transcribe an entire tape, listen to it and jot down the important parts on a SOURCE DATA SHEET. You can then review this sheet to formulate your questions. Or, for even more of a short cut, write your questions on a Q & A SHEET while you're listening to the tape. You probably won't write as many questions using this method but they may be adequate for your particular purpose.

Surveys

A quick way to compile a list of questions for the categories you have selected is to do a survey of common information. We have included three sample surveys (figures 9, 10, & 11) you can use to get more information on weddings, births or sports. You will find that the information you get from these surveys will help you develop questions for other categories as well, such as: Statistics, Entertainment, and Special Occasions. Also, if you are researching your family tree, the answers you receive from a wedding and/or birth survey (such as maiden names) will certainly help you.

Tailor your survey to fit your particular needs. We asked relatives who participated in a team sport to complete a sports survey (figure 11) and if they competed in more than one team sport we asked them to complete additional surveys.

You can create similar surveys. The subject will depend on your informational needs or the categories in your game.

Don't overlook those close friends who can give you an incredible amount of good information about family members. Also, contact long-distance friends or relatives whom you haven't seen for awhile. Neighbors from an old neighborhood could also offer forgotten anecdotes. Simply call or write to them explaining what you're doing and the kind of information you need, then send them a questionnaire and a self-addressed stamped envelope. Ask them to fill it out and add their comments.

What a great way to establish lost contact and to renew old relationships with friends and family!

Figure 9

INTERVIEW SURVEY -- WEDDINGS

Name of Person Completing Survey: _____

Date:_____

Full Names of Bride & Groom:_____

Date of Wedding:_____

No. in Attendance:_____

No. of Bridesmaids:_____

No. of Ushers:_____

Officiator's Name:_____

Flower Girl's Name:_____

Ring Bearer's Name:_____

Where was the reception held?_____

Who was the best man?_____

Who was the maid of honor?_____

What colors did the bridesmaids wear?_____

Who caught the bouquet?_____

Who caught the garter?_____

What was the name of the band?_____

What was the name of the first song the couple danced to?

_____

Where did the couple go on their honeymoon?

_____

How long was their honeymoon?_____

Figure 10

INTERVIEW SURVEY -- BIRTHS

Name of Person Completing Survey:_____
Date:_____

	NAME	DATE	PLACE	WGT
1st Child				
2nd Child				
3rd Child				
You				
Spouse				
Mother				
Father				
Paternal G'father				
Paternal G'mother				
Maternal G'father				
Maternal G'mother				
Paternal Gr/G'father				
Paternal Gr/G'mother				
Maternal Gr/G'father				
Paternal Gr/G'mother				
Paternal Gr/Gr/G'father				
Paternal Gr/Gr/G'mother				
Maternal Gr/Gr/G'father				
Maternal Gr/Gr/G'mother				

68

Figure 11

INTERVIEW SURVEY -- SPORTS

Name of Person Completing Survey:_____
Date:_____

Name of Sport:_____

Year(s) of Participation:_____

Position(s) Played:_____

Most Points (Runs, Goals, etc.) Scored in One Game:_____

Least Points (Runs, Goals, etc.) Scored in One Game:_____

Name of Coach:_____

Name of Team:_____

Number on Uniform:_____

Color of Uniform:_____

Nickname of Team:_____

Awards/Recognitions:_____

Outstanding Memory:

_____

_____

_____

_____

Two Teammates and Their Positions:_____

Win/Loss Record:_____

CHAPTER 10

Incorporating Photography, Art, And Audio-Visual Equipment

Getting started

One of the most rewarding parts of researching and writing *IT'S ALL RELATIVE* for your family is its creative aspect. This creativity can easily expand beyond the basic research and writing stage to include photography, art, and audio-visual equipment. No you don't have to be a professional photographer, artist, or audio-visual expert to accomplish this. All you need is enthusiasm, access to some basic equipment, and perhaps a drawing pencil or two.

Because it's not necessary to use any special equipment in your game, the following lists are strictly optional, but if you do have access to any of these materials or equipment, please consider expanding your game through their use - as we explain in this chapter.

Materials: family photos (antique to present) - family slides - family home movies - family trinkets - letter-size envelopes - markers - construction paper - scissors - film

Equipment: 35mm camera - videocamera - slide projector - slide viewer - movie projector - movie screen - tape recorder/cassette player

Incorporating Family Photography

Family photographs contain invaluable historical clues because they capture both events and feelings in a moment. Any photographs you have available, from the past to the present, can add another unique aspect to your version of *IT'S ALL RELATIVE*.

Photography was invented in 1839, but it wasn't until 1888 that Kodak brought out the first box camera which brought the camera out of the studio. Morever, until the 1920's, daily activities weren't often captured on film so chances are that you'll have few family photographs, with the exception of official portraits, available before this time.

The easiest way to incorporate photography into your game is to place family photographs (which may range from current snapshots to historical daguerreotypes depending on your game's focus) one by one in individual letter-size envelopes, and assign a code to each envelope. Or in lieu of envelopes, you may want to construct personalized jackets from construction paper for each picture. Then, keeping in mind that *everything* in the frame counts, brainstorm a list of questions for each photograph: What are the full names of each person in this picture? - What event were these people attending? - What year is it? - What kind of car is in the background?

Later, when you transfer your questions to the Q & A CARDS, jot the code number on the question side of the card so the player knows which envelope he or she needs to answer that particular question.

You may even want to use "pictures" as a separate category in your game, or you may choose to intersperse questions related to the pictures among all your categories. (See CHAPTER 3: Selecting Categories.)

If you don't want to remove pictures from photo albums, or if you don't own some of the pictures you'd like to use, one alternative is to use a photocopier. The quality of the copies is certainly adequate for your purposes, and it's significantly less expensive than your other alternative which is to have reprints made. Also, it protects the original pictures from damage or loss. (Be cautious, however, about photocopying antique photographs because they need to be handled with care and shouldn't be overexposed to light.)

If you do choose reprints, try to locate the negatives as these will produce the best quality. However, this may be difficult because most people don't have their negatives readily available or organized so your best choice may be to have prints made directly from the pictures. In that case, consider using a mail order film processing company. Their rates are usually much less than general photography stores. To ensure reliability however, choose a company you've previously used. Also, it makes sense not to send everything in one mailing. This way if your pictures are lost or misplaced, you won't lose everything.

Naturally if you want prints from antique or cherished photos, or if you're using someone else's pictures, you'd be wise to take your business to a local photography store with an established reputation.

Incorporating family slides

If you have slides you want to use in your game, you have three choices. You can have prints made from them and follow the same procedure; you can individually number the slides themselves, put them in separate envelopes, and use a small slide viewer during the game, or you can project them and use a 35 mm camera to take pictures from this projection.

Photographing projected images will require some experimentation. Work in a darkened room and set your camera on a tripod behind the projector and as close to the same axis of the projector as possible.

If possible, project the image onto a flat white surface, and not a screen because this will avoid reflections.

If you are using a single reflex 35 mm camera, use the light meter to take a reading of the projected image and adjust your settings accordingly. You should use a fairly slow shutter speed, and your image may be more sharply defined if you use a telephoto lens.

If you're using a 35 mm automatic camera as we did, use 1000 ASA film. With an automatic camera, the picture quality may be diminished because you don't have as much flexibility as you do with a standard 35 mm camera, but with a little ingenuity and practice, you can take pictures which will be suitable for your purposes, even if they're not perfect photographs.

Incorporating home movies

You can also convert frames from home movies into snapshots. Use a projector with freeze-frame capacity and follow the above procedures. The game players will probably be amazed and amused to see themselves in these "new" pictures.

And the questions you can write from them are bound to be interesting and funny.

Incorporating family video tapes

Because video cameras have basically replaced movie cameras, many families are now video-taping their family events. You can also transfer these video images to film by setting your VCR on "pause" and taking "pictures" directly from the TV screen.

Or you can create a video tape which is a compilation of home movies, pictures, and slides, and key your questions to the numbers on the counter of the VCR.

If you own a video camera, you can do this yourself with the aid of a special copy screen (available in photography stores). If you don't own your own equipment, many places offer video transfer as a service.

Other photographic possibilities

Another photographic activity is to make a duplicate of a picture and then cut the duplicate into sections, like a puzzle.

You can use a regular size picture, but it may be more fun if you have it enlarged first and then put the individual pieces into separate envelopes and code them just as with the other photographs and slides.

Have the players identify: this mustache – these eyes – this nose – these lips – this outfit – this scene – the date.

These visual questions are guaranteed to provide lots of laughs and interesting conversations during the game. You may even want to have the players use a magnifying glass to assist them in these identifications.

You might also consider having some photographs actually made into puzzles, a service some photography stores and companies provide. Include the puzzle pieces in an envelope, either individually or as a group. If you do this individually, the set-up will be identical to the above. But if you include all the pieces in one envelope, you can design the question(s) so the player has an answering time limit as he attempts to piece the puzzle together.

Another photographic activity is to actually take pictures of antiques, memorabilia, and any of the treasures mentioned in CHAPTER 6: Searching Your Family Archives And Treasures. Include these pictures in coded envelopes and write related questions just as with the other pictures.

A related activity is to gather several small family trinkets (membership cards, pins, rings, campaign buttons, knick-knacks, hair ribbons, tie tacks, charms, etc.) and either photograph, or place them in a "treasure bag" which will become part of your game. Again, code each item and key your questions to the code.

Incorporating artwork

If you're artistic, you can sketch family events, mementos, house designs, family portraits, caricatures, maps, scenes from the past, and family cartoons, and again follow the procedure of placing them in an envelope and coding them. If you're lacking artistic ability, then limit your drawings to stick figures. Remember the purpose is to have fun and to add an extra dimension to *IT'S ALL RELATIVE*, not to test your artistic or photographic abilities.

Organizing photographs and artwork

You need containers to hold the above photographic and artistic activities. Three large, different-colored index card file boxes will make it easy for you to organize your envelopes. Place photographs in one, slides in another, and artwork in the third. (For further information on creating containers for your game, see CHAPTER 11: Writing The Game.)

Incorporating an "audio" category

Game shows frequently include an "audio" category. You can do the same for your game. Use the counter on a cassette or reel-to-reel tape recorder as your numbering guide for each segment of your audio questions. Again key your questions to each segment so that the player listens to a designated part of the tape and answers a question related to it.

Preparing the tapes requires a lot of time, but it will be worth it because of the unique aspect it will add to your game. Consider these possibilities: Use voices from old family tapes, family movies, or family videos. - Start saving the messages your family leaves on your answering machine and transferring them onto a game tape. - Record parts of meaningful television shows or songs. (See CHAPTER 4: Brainstorming for more information on connecting songs to family history and trivia.)

Use any or all of the ideas we've suggested in this chapter and your game will be lively, creative, and intense. Furthermore, your family will be delighted by these unexpected personal aspects of your family's history. What better way to document and preserve your heritage?

CHAPTER 11

Writing The Game

General information

After you've completed as much research as you feel is necessary, it's time to get down to the nitty-gritty: writing questions and answers for your game.

First review your SOURCE DATA SHEETS and use this information to write all possible questions and answers onto the Q & A SHEETS. Even if some of your questions don't make sense, leave them for now. You may be able to rewrite them and use them later.

Be sure to note the code number from the SOURCE DATA SHEETS onto the Q & A SHEETS in case you need clarification on a question or answer later.

Keep questions relatively short and to the point. For instance, don't write a question such as, "What happened during Cameron's 1982 summer vacation?", because there are several possible answers. Instead, write, "What event nearly ruined Cameron's 1982 summer vacation?" The answer, "He broke his hand" is specific and much less apt to be disputed by the game players than an answer to the first question would have been. (See "Answer Disputes" in CHAPTER 12: Game Rules.)

When you write your questions and answers, you have to decide what names you'll use. This sounds simpler than it is. For our first version of the game, we used "Mom" and "Dad" when we referred to our parents - which was fine, because the focus of our game then was our immediate family. However, if you consider your game to be a family legacy, you should use complete names for the sake of clarity for future generations.

Most of your questions will be written in the form of fill-ins, short answers, and identifications. To add more variety to your questions and answers, phrase some of them as multiple choice, or true and false. Multiple choice questions can be difficult or easy, but either way they'll liven up your game.

With true and false questions, you can have fun writing true questions that no one will believe - or making up questions you've always wanted to be true.

Categories

Although the game is designed for up to eight different categories, we suggest that you select only four to start because it's simpler and less frustrating to develop questions for fewer categories. You should write a minimum of fifty questions for each category; seventy-five to one hundred are preferable.

You can always add categories later. For example, in our second version of *IT'S ALL RELATIVE*, we enlisted family help with writing questions and answers by having four "couples" categories (Mom and Dad, Lynn and Bob, Lorna and John, Kim and Cam). A few weeks before Christmas, we asked each individual to write ten questions and answers about themselves, ten about their relationship as couples, and five (or more) questions about the other couples. We instructed them to include only questions relating to 1983-1987.

This "category" experiment worked very well. We learned new information about each other, we updated our game, and we started a family tradition of playing *IT'S ALL RELATIVE* on Christmas Eve. And best of all, there were plenty of questions that we, as the original creators of our game, didn't know the answers to!

Game pieces

The game pieces at the back of the book include:

Game letters: 16 I's, 16 T's, 8 S's, 16 A's, 24 L's, 8 R's, 8 V's, 16 E's.
Four personal game boards that spell *IT'S ALL RELATIVE*.

You will need to create Q & A CARDS by cutting colored paper to a convenient size or by purchasing colored 3x5 index cards. (If you do not wish to have categories, you may use plain white paper or white 3x5 index cards.)

Cut two 1x1-inch squares from each color category. These game pieces determine which category of questions the player will be answering. (If you are playing without categories, you do not need to prepare game pieces.)

Procedures

Determine your game's categories, as explained in CHAPTER 3. Write the name of the categories and their corresponding colors on the reference charts. Players will refer to these reference charts during the game.

After you've written your categories and colors on the coded reference charts, look at the first category. Let's say it's "Statistics" and its corresponding color is pink. Use a fine point pink marker and review your Q & A SHEETS for questions fitting this category. Highlight them in pink.

If your second category is "Entertainment" and its corresponding color is blue, follow the above procedure with a blue marker.

After you've completed this process with all your categories (up to eight) you are ready to transfer your questions to the Q & A CARDS.

Write your "Statistics" questions (one to a card) near the top of one side of the 3x5 cards and write the answer near the bottom of the other side of the card. (Try to write a minimum of fifty questions per category.)

Game piece containers

Because this game is in book form, you need containers for the game letters, game pieces, and the Q & A CARDS.* This is where your ingenuity, regardless of your artistic ability, can truly personalize your game. Some ideas: Decorate a shoe box, kleenex box, coffee can - Construct a wooden container - Create a ceramic container - Decorate a manila envelope or paper bag - Sew a cloth drawstring bag - Use plastic food containers.

*For our original version of *IT'S ALL RELATIVE* we used 2 baby wipe containers, one for the game letters, and one for the game pieces, and we cut miniature cereal boxes in half to hold our Q & A CARDS. These items may have lacked sentimental value, but they were inexpensive and easy to come by. And what's inside is a priceless heirloom our family will treasure now and for generations to come.

You can personalize any of the above containers using basic art supplies (pens, markers, paints, etc.) and with such coverings as leftover wallpaper, copies of old newspapers or magazine pages, contact paper, or even simple construction paper. And the drawstring bag could be sewn from leftover material or a family member's old curtains, bedspreads, or clothes.

If you don't wish to take the time to decorate a container, you should consider using a family heirloom such as a jar, metal box, strongbox, jewelry box, cigar box, hat box, Christmas box, cookie tin, pantry box, wooden salt box, portable letter writing desk, button box, snuff box, or whatever.

Even if you don't have the time, talent, or means to create a fancy container, don't worry: it's what's inside that counts!

CHAPTER 12

Game Rules

IT'S ALL RELATIVE is a game for two to eight players or teams. The object of the game is to spell the words *IT'S All RELATIVE* by correctly answering questions.

To begin

Distribute a personal game board to each player or team. Turn all game letters face down, or pour them into a container, and place them in the middle of the playing area.

Place the 16 game pieces in another container. Each game piece is color-coded to represent a category which has been assigned by the writer(s) of the game.

Place the Q & A CARDS in containers organized by category, question side facing forward.

The play

Each player or team blindly draws one letter from the middle of the playing area and places it, right side up, on his personal game board. The player, drawing the letter nearest the beginning of the alphabet plays first. (In the event of more than one person drawing the same letter closest to the front of the alphabet, these players return their letters to the pile and draw again to determine who starts the game. The rest of the players do not return their letters or draw again.)

Each player or team begins play with one letter on the game board.

When the first player has been determined, he blindly draws a playing piece from that container. The color of that piece determines the category of the question he's to answer.

Another player reads the question aloud to him. If the player answers the question correctly, he blindly selects a letter from the playing area, and places it right side up on the corresponding letter on his personal game board. Play then resumes to the left.

If he answers the question incorrectly, he does not draw a letter. Either way, play resumes to the left and the Q & A CARD is placed in the back of the pile.

The game continues until a player or team wins by filling his game board with game pieces spelling *IT'S ALL RELATIVE*.

Special notes

Duplicate Letters: In the event that a player draws a letter that he does not need (for instance, a second "V"), he may

(1) keep the letter, or
(2) return the letter face-down to the playing area and draw another letter. However, to do this, he must also take a blank Q & A CARD and write a new question and answer for the game. He may write this question and answer at *any time* during the play of the game, but he cannot win the game if he holds any blank Q & A CARDS. After he's written the question and answer, he places his Q & A CARD in *front* of the appropriate category so that it will be drawn during this play of the game.

Strategy: A player may swap a duplicate letter for a new letter and a blank Q & A CARD at any time during the game – or he may decide to keep his duplicate letters so he can limit another player's/team's ability to collect the necessary letters to win.

Answer Disputes: The current player may disagree with an answer. If he can convince the majority of players that his answer is correct, the Q & A CARD is rewritten and placed in the back of the appropriate category in the Q & A container. Then the current player may draw a game letter and play continues to the left.

If the current player is unable to convince the majority of players that his answer is correct, the Q & A CARD remains as written, the current player does not draw a game letter, and play resumes to the left.

Players other than the current player may disagree with an answer, but it will have no effect on the current player's turn – even if it's determined that the answer on the card is incorrect.

Suggestions For Players: The first time you play *IT'S ALL RELATIVE*, it's important that you explain the purpose of the game to your family members. Remind them to think of the game as a time capsule, a capsule which includes a little bit of everything and which needs to be opened occasionally so its contents can be updated for future generations.

Explain that as family members and players of the game, they have a responsibility to add to it by writing their own questions and answers because their knowledge, family connections, perspectives, and feelings are unique. Reassure them that as the original creator of the game, you share the same responsibility.

As explained in the rules, the game allows players to write new questions as part of the winning strategy. First-time players may feel uncomfortable with this so it's up to you to demonstrate how simple and fun this can be.

Point out that a number of new question ideas probably will strike them just by playing the game and that just one question: What was John's favoirte sport?, is bound to bring several other related questions to mind, such as: When did John start this sport? How many teams has John played on? How many injuries has John received while playing this sport?

Remind them that the question possibilities are almost endless, and that if they start with the obvious such as looking at their hands and thinking about the history behind a ring or a scar, or if they look around the room and create questions based on their surroundings, they'll discover that they, too, can write questions for *IT'S ALL RELATIVE*.

Finally, remind the players that this is a *trivia* game and that the only dumb question is the one they don't add to their family history.

STATISTICS

SAMPLE QUESTIONS

How much did ?'s first house cost?

How many rooms in ?'s house?

How many fireplaces in ?'s house?

What year did ? build their addition? pool? garage?

How many square feet in ?'s house?

How many times has ? moved?

What did ? pay for monthly rent in (year)?

What was the interest rate on ?'s first mortgage?

What was the year and make of ?'s first car?

How many traffic violations has ? had?

What's the license number of ?'s car?

How many car accidents has ? had?

How many car accidents have been ?'s fault?

How old were ?'s parents when they met? married? divorced? died?

How much did ?'s engagement ring cost? wedding gown? wedding?

What time was ?'s wedding?, graduation?

How many attendants in ?'s wedding?

How many guests at ?'s wedding?

How long did ?'s marriage last?

How much alimony did ? have to pay?

Give the total number of marriages for ?, ?, and ?.

How many stepchildren does ? have?

During her pregnancy, how much weight did ? gain?

What was ?'s birth weight? height? time of birth?

How many hours was ? in labor with ?.

What's the age difference between ? and ? ?

In what year was ? twice as old as ? ?

How old was ? when she wore her first bra? First date?

How much was ?'s first allowance?

How many students in ?'s graduating class?

How many years was ? a Girl Scout? Campfire Girl? Boy Scout? Cub Scout?

How much was ? paid per hour for his first job?

How old was ? when she had her first kiss?

What is the most ? has ever weighed?

How many different colors has ?'s hair been?

At what age did ? start smoking? Stop smoking?

How many cavities has ? had?

What's ?'s blood type?

In (year), what was ?'s cholesterol level? blood pressure?

How old was ? at his death?

How many times has ? been on an airplane? train? boat?

How many times has ? been out of state?

How many years did ? take singing lessons? piano? dancing? tennis?

In what year did ? graduate from high school? College?

How many stitches did ? have in his foot? lip? arm?

How many bones has ? broken?

How old was ? when he got a hearing aid?

What's the most ? has ever paid for a dress? suit? bottle of wine? dinner? hotel room?

Within 5 pounds, what is the difference between ?'s birth weight and current weight?

How many years has ? worked at _____ ?

How old was ? when she/he got braces?

How long did ? wear braces?

How many wisdom teeth did ? have removed at one time?

What was ?'s draft card number?

How many credit cards does ? have?

How many cords of wood did ? buy in (year)?

How tall is ? ?

What size shoe does ? wear?

What is the most ? ever won playing the lottery?

What are the first 3 digits of ?'s Social Security number?

What turnpike exit number does ? take to get to work?

ENTERTAINMENT

SAMPLE QUESTIONS

Where did ? and ? go on their first date?

What is ? and ?'s song?

During their courtship, what was ? and ?'s favorite Saturday activity?

What's ?'s favorite beverage?

What did ? give ? for a wedding gift?

When did ? lose his virginity?

What's ?'s nickname?

Where did ? celebrate her --th birthday?

Where did ? meet ? ?

What's ?'s favorite restaurant?

With whom did ? go on a blind date?

What was ? doing when she/he met ? for the first time?

Who sang at ?'s wedding?

Who was the flower girl at ?'s wedding?

What's ?'s favorite vacation spot?

Where did ? go on a cruise?

In (year), what country did ? visit?

What movie did ? and ? see at the drive in?

What movie star would ? most like to meet?

What's ?'s favorite movie?

Who is ?'s favorite comedian?

When ? was (age), who was his favorite rock star?

Whose autograph does ? have?

What famous person does ? resemble?

Who's the most famous person ? has ever met? ever seen?

Who would ? say is the funniest person he knows?

What song did ?'s senior class sing at graduation?

What person in our family knows how to square dance? limbo? play an instrument? tap dance?

Who took dance lessons? singing?

What was the name of the character ? played in the 6th grade play?

What instrument did ? play in the high school band?

What solo did ? play in the high school band?

What piece did ? recite at his graduation?

What was the name of ?'s fraternity? sorority?

What's ?'s best talent?

What outfit did ? wear for his first Halloween?

In (year) what was ?'s favorite TV show?

Who is ?'s favorite soap opera star?

In (year) what TV show did ? hate?

What play did ? see in (year)?

Who did ? see in concert in (year)?

What lullabye did ? sing to his/her children?

What's ?'s favorite board game?

What song did ? sing at ?'s wedding?

What's ?'s astrological sign?

What's ?'s favorite ice cream?

What is the brand name of ?'s VCR? stereo? camera? skiis?

Of ?, ?, and ?, who has never talked to a fortune teller?

How often does ? go to a tanning salon?

What is ?'s favorite place to shop?

What instruments does ? play?

What TV show does ? always tape?

What game show would ? love to be on?

In (year), who went on vacation with ? ?

True or False: ? once wanted to marry ? ?

Who arrived late to ?'s wedding? graduation? funeral?

What was ?'s favorite bar/pub in (year)?

What was the name of the family ? babysat for Tuesday nights in (year)?

True or False: ? once ate 3 Big Macs in 10 minutes.

Name the dog ? took to obedience school.

What is ?'s favorite magazine?

What was the name of ?'s college dormitory?

What is the name of ?'s cable company?

Where does ? rent movies?

SPORTS

SAMPLE QUESTIONS

What color was ?'s first bicycle?

How many bicycles has ? owned?

How old was ? when she learned to ride a bicycle?

What was ?'s batting average in high school?

What were the most points ? scored in a high school basketball game?

What's the slowest time ? ever ran the mile in college?

What's the most weight ? has ever bench pressed?

What horsepower was ?'s boat motor?

How many sports trophies has ? won?

In (year), what size bathing suit did ? wear?

What grade was ? in when he won his first blue ribbon?

What year did ? shoot her first deer?

How much did the deer weigh?

What was ?'s favorite basketball team? (baseball, football, hockey, etc.)

What was the name of ?'s Little League team?

What position did ? play on the basketball team? (baseball, football, hockey, etc.)

What sport(s) did ? play in grade school? high school? college?

What sport did ? try out for and not make the team?

What was the name of the team ? coached?

93

How did ? react when Ted Williams hit his 1941 All Star homer? When the Red Sox lost the World Series?

In high school, how many miles did ? run weekly?

Who's the fastest runner on ?'s side of the family?

What's ?'s favorite brand of sneakers?

What's ?'s favorite sport to play?

What's ?'s favorite sport to watch?

? was injured playing what sport?

What was ?'s most embarrassing moment in sports?

Why did ? give up (name of sport)?

What's the name of the first mountain ? ever skiied?

Which of ?'s boyfriends/girlfriends was most athletic?

What friend(s) did ? go sailing with? camping? hiking? biking?

What color, make and model was ?'s first speedboat?

Of ?, ?, and ?, who is the best waterskiier? snowskiier? bowler? golfer? tennis player?

How many fishing poles does ? own?

Where does ? buy his bait?

Where's ?'s favorite fishing hole?

Of ?, ? and ?, who did <u>not</u> take swimming lessons? other lessons?

What's the most number of fish ? caught in one day?

What's the name of ?'s fitness club?

What's the yearly membership cost at ?'s fitness club?

What is the maximum number of miles ? has ridden her exercise bike at one time?

What's the name of the campground ? goes to each summer?

Where did ? buy her camper?

How many people does ?'s camper sleep?

In what swimming event does ? excel?

What's the number on ?'s racing car?

What is the name of ?'s motorcycle club?

Who gave ? his/her first tennis racket? skiis? basketball?

Why did ? hate to play softball? basketball? soccer?

Of ?, ?, and ?, who did not go on the canoe trip in (year)?

True or False: ? can't swim. waterski. ride a bike.

How old was ? when he stopped playing rugby?

Who was the pitcher on ?'s baseball team? catcher?

Of ?, ?, and ?, who has not been in a hot air balloon?

What is ?'s highest bowling score?

What is ?'s golf handicap?

What was ?'s highest rating in diving competition?

What is the most number of gaols ? scored in soccer in one game in (year)?

How old was ? when he started playing ice hockey?

Of ?, ?, and ?, who owns a kayak?

What is the name of the speedway where ? races?

What sport was ? playing when he broke his finger? leg? collar bone?

MISCELLANEOUS

SAMPLE QUESTIONS

What dress was ? wearing the night she met ? ?

What outfit did ? wear to (special occasion)?

What color was ?'s first sofa?

What color are ?'s contacts tinted?

What was the first name of ?'s first grade teacher? dentist? hygienist? doctor? hair dresser? boss? minister?

If ? had been a girl (boy), what would ?'s name have been?

How do you spell ?'s last name?

Name in order all the animals ? has owned.

In (year) what was ?'s paperboy's name?

What was the name of ?'s cat? dog? horse?

What was ?'s favorite toy?

When ? died, who was President? Governor?

When ? was born, who was President? Governor?

What presidents were elected during ?'s lifetime?

What was ?'s worst cooking disaster?

What kind of cake does ? always have on her birthday?

How does ? like to have her eggs cooked?

What food(s) is ? allergic to?

What food does ? hate?

Name three vegetables in ?'s garden.

What medicine is ? allergic to?

What rock group/singer did ? see in concert in (year)?

What newspapers does ? read daily?

What's ?'s favorite magazine?

What does ? say is ?'s worst habit?

What's ?'s real hair color?

What was ?'s most embarrassing moment?

If ? could change anything about her body, what would it be?

What contests has ? been in?

Where did ? get her first kiss?

What religious denomination is ? ?

Where was ? baptized?

How many times has ? been to the emergency room?

In (year) what was ?'s monthly mortgage payment?

What's ?'s favorite fruit?

How many years did ? attend college?

What year did ? get his college degree?

In (year), what was ?'s telephone number?

In (year), what street did ?'s best friend live on?

How much was a Hershey Bar in 1963?

At what bank did ? open her first savings account?

Where did ? and ? spend the first night of their honeymoon?

What do ? and ? argue about the most?

97

What was the cause of ?'s death?

Where was ?'s funeral held?

Why didn't ? go to ?'s funeral?

How does ? take his coffee?

What is ?'s favorite kind of coffee?

What college degree(s) does ? have?

Who pierced ?'s ears?

Which class office did ? hold in college?

Of ?, ?, and ?, which one had a c-section?

Where does ? breakfast most of the time?

Of ?, ?, and ?, who does not have any cavities?

Who hasn't been to the dentist since (year)?

What branch of the Armed Services did ? serve?

What war did ? serve in?

What was ?'s highest rank in the Army? Navy? Coast Guard?

True or False: ? was born in (city).

True or False: It rained on ?'s wedding day.

What's the name of ?'s bank?

In what month did ? move to his/her present house?

What is the name of ?'s Day Care Center?

What is the sum of the digits in ?'s phone number?

BIBLIOGRAPHY

Alessi, Jean, Jan Miller. *Once Upon A Memory*. White Hall, Virginia:Betterway Publications, Inc., 1987.

Beard, Timothy Field, Denise Demong. *How To Find Your Family Roots*. New York:McGraw-Hill Book Co., 1977.

Bronson, Fred. *The Billboard Book of Number One Hits*. New York:Billboard Publications, Inc., 1985.

Brooks, Tim, Earle Marsh. *The Complete Directory To Prime Time Network TV Shows*. New York:Ballantine Books, 1985.

Curruth, Gorton (ed.). *The Encyclopedia of American Facts and Dates*. New York:Thomas Y. Crowell Company, 1972.

Crandall, Ralph. *Shaking Your Family Tree*. Dublin, New Hampshire:Yankee Publishing Inc., 1986.

Croom, Emily Anne. *Unpuzzling Your Past*. White Hall, Virginia:Betterway Publications, Inc., 1983.

Doane, Gilbert H., James B. Bell. *Searching For Your Ancestors*. Minneapolis:University of Minnesota Press, 1986.

Felkner, Bruce C. *How To Look Things Up and Find Things Out*. New York:William Morrow Company, 1988.

Fletcher, William. *Recording Your Family History*. New York:Dodd, Mead & Company, 1986.

Greenwood, Val D. *The Researcher's Guide to American Genealogy*. Baltimore:Genealogical Publishing Co., Inc., 1977

Helmbold, F. Wilbur. *Tracing Your Ancestry*. Birmingham, Alabama:Oxmoor House, Inc., 1976.

Hofmann, William J. *Life Writing: A Guide to Family Journals and Personal Memoirs*. New York:St. Martin's Press, 1982.

99

Huberman, Ron, Laura Janis. *Video Family Portraits.* Bowie, Maryland: Heritage Books, Inc., 1987.

Jones, Vincent L., Arlene H. Eakle, Mildred K. Christensen. *Family History For Fun and Profit.* Provo, Utah:Genealogical Copy Service, 1972.

Monke, Frank. *The Encyclopedia Of Sports.* New York:A. S. Barnes and Company, 1969.

Michael, Paul (ed.). *The Great American Movie Book.* Englewood Cliffs, New Jersey:Prentice-Hall, 1980.

"Military Service Records in the National Archives of the United States." Washington, D.C.:National Archives and Records Administration, 1985.

Mitz, Rick. *The Great TV Sitcom Book.* New York:Richard Marek Publishers, 1980.

Noren, Catherine. *The Way We Looked: The Meaning and Magic of Family Photographs.* New York:Lodestar Books, 1983.

Stevenson, Noel C. *Search and Research.* Salt Lake City:Deseret Book Company, 1979.

Stryker-Rodda, Harriet. *How To Climb Your Family Tree.* Baltimore:Genealogical Publishing Co., 1983.

Trager, James. *The People's Chronology: A Year-by-Year Record of Human Events From Prehistory to the Present.* New York:Holt, Rinehart, and Winston, 1979.

"Using Records in the National Archives for Genealogical Research". Washington, D.C.:National Archives and Records Administration, 1986.

Westin, Jeane Eddy. *Finding Your Roots.* Los Angeles:J. P. Tarcher, Inc., 1977.

The Way To Play: The Illustrated Encyclopedia of the Games of the World. New York:Paddington Press Ltd., 1975.

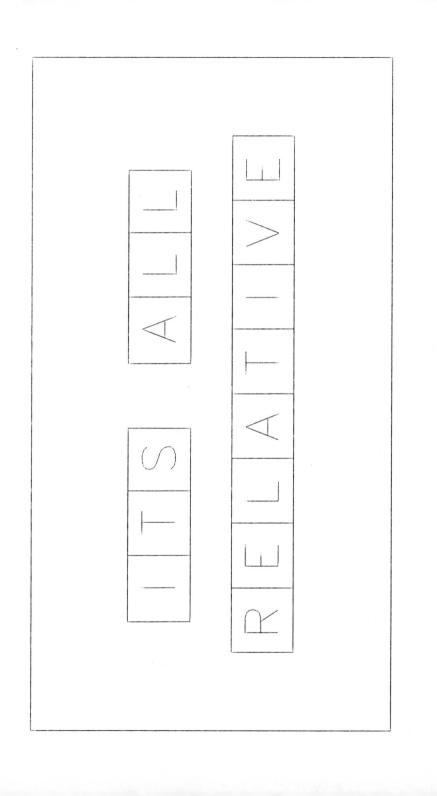

ITS ALL
RELATIVE

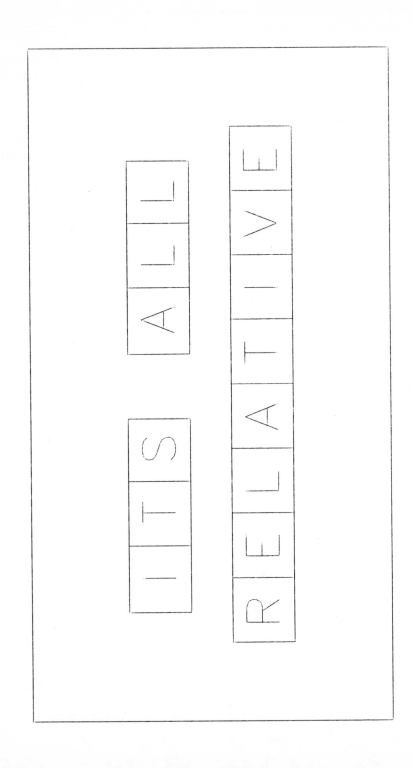

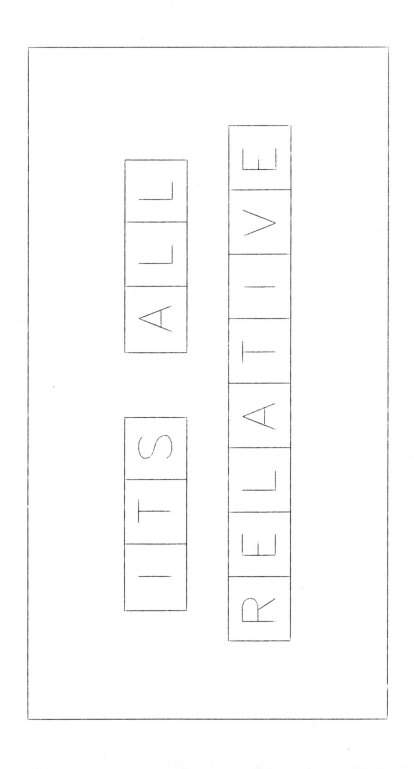

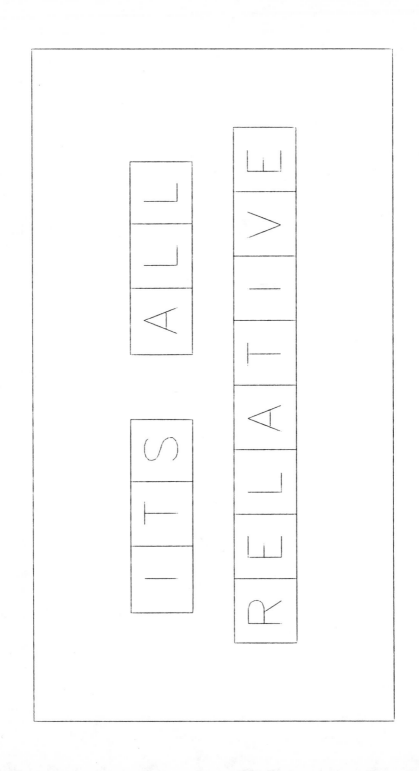

ITS ALL

RELATIVE

REFERENCE CHART

COLOR   CATEGORY NAME

1. _____

2. _____

3. _____

4. _____

5. _____

6. _____

7. _____

8. _____

FOLD

REFERENCE CHART

COLOR   CATEGORY NAME

1. _____

2. _____

3. _____

4. _____

5. _____

6. _____

7. _____

8. _____

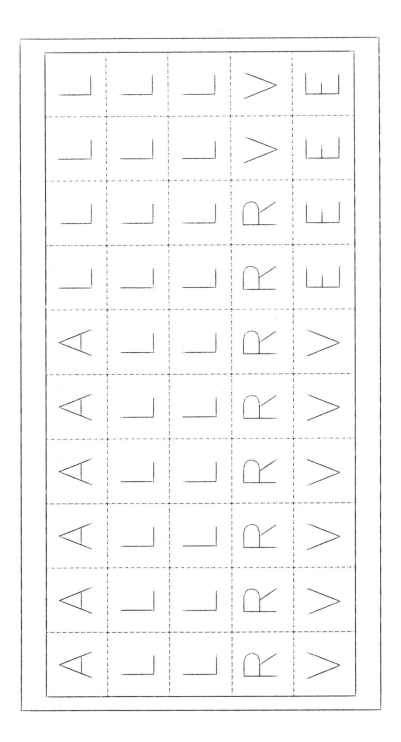

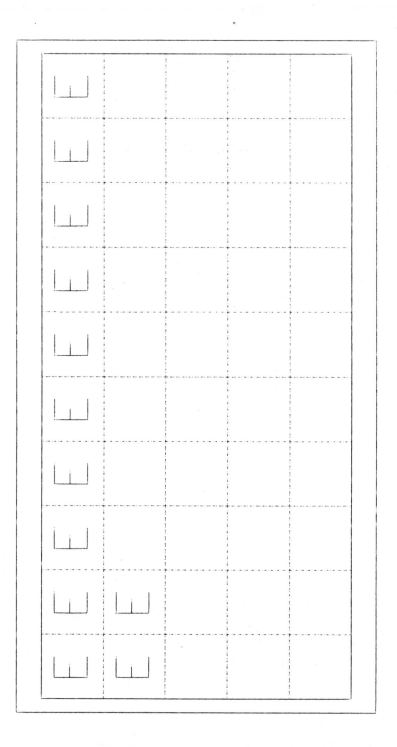